THE ULTIMATE

How to find constellations and read the night sky like a pro

GUIDE TO THE SKY

By John Mosley, program supervisor for
Griffith Observatory, Los Angeles, California

Illustrated by Carol Lyon

LOWELL HOUSE JUVENILE

LOS ANGELES

CONTEMPORARY BOOKS

CHICAGO

To Jack
—J. M.

Publisher: Jack Artenstein
Director of Publishing Services: Rena Copperman
Executive Managing Editor, Juvenile Division: Brenda Pope-Ostrow
Editor in Chief, Lowell House Juvenile: Amy Downing
Art Director: Lisa-Theresa Lenthall
Typesetter: Carolyn Wendt
Cover Design and Art: Justin Segal

Library of Congress Catalog Card Number is available.

ISBN: 1-56565-596-6

Lowell House books can be purchased at special discounts when ordered in bulk for premiums and special sales. Contact Department TC at the following address:

Lowell House Juvenile
2020 Avenue of the Stars, Suite 300
Los Angeles, CA 90067

Manufactured in the United States of America
10 9 8 7 6 5 4 3 2

CONTENTS

INTRODUCTION: **So You Want to Study the Stars?**

5

CHAPTER 1: **Stargazing Basics**

6

CHAPTER 2: **How to Use This Book**

13

CHAPTER 3: **The Constellations**

18

CHAPTER 4: **The Star Charts**

67

CHAPTER 5: **What to Do Next?**

76

GLOSSARY

78

INDEX

80

SO YOU WANT TO STUDY THE STARS?

There are literally billions of stars in the sky, and every one of them belongs to one of the 88 constellations. The constellations are your key to finding your way around the sky.

It is not hard to learn the constellations, and you certainly don't have to memorize all 88! Many minor constellations contain only faint stars and are not important. Others are too far south to be seen from your home. If you learn the major constellations—those with bright stars—you will know the sky very well, and you can learn the other ones later if you wish.

The constellations change with the seasons, so it takes most of one year to learn them. It doesn't matter when you start. At any instant you can see half the sky, and if you watch all night, you can see roughly two-thirds of the sky. However, you cannot see stars in the part of the sky that is now behind the sun. To see those stars you must wait until the sun no longer blocks them, and that takes a few months.

Take one full year to learn the major constellations. In the second year you can reacquaint yourself with them. In the third year the constellations will be old friends, and you will feel like an expert stargazer as you point them out to *your* friends. But you need not stop learning. There are enough faint stars to keep you busy for a lifetime! And if you use binoculars or a telescope, you will find many other objects among the stars, such as star clusters and nebulae.

This book will help you identify the constellations. You will learn about their histories, and you will find out why you see certain constellations at different times of night and in different seasons. The best thing is, once you learn the constellations, you will remember them the rest of your life.

John Mosley

CHAPTER 1

STARGAZING BASICS

If you do not know any constellations, the sky can be a confusing place. So, before you head outside with your Rotating Star Finder and star charts, read about what a constellation is and how knowing them can help you find your way easily around the sky.

What is a constellation?

A constellation is not only a pattern of stars, but it is also a specific area of the sky and includes everything that lies within its boundaries. Think of a state (or province, if you are in Canada). Each state has its boundaries, and everything within those boundaries is part of that state. The boundaries of the constellations were decided by a committee of astronomers in 1928, and these boundaries are shown on some star charts. Everything in the sky—whether a star, nebula, or galaxy—is in one constellation or another.

If you look at a star chart—especially an old one—you will see fancy figures like ladies in flowing robes and an animal that is half-goat and half-fish. These figures were added long ago by artists who wanted to beautify their star charts, but you won't find (and should not look for) such fancy characters in the sky. Look instead for simple patterns of stars such as crosses, squares, triangles, circles, and bent lines. These lines and patterns may not be official, but using them makes it easy to learn the constellations. You can even make up your own patterns if they help you find your way.

A few constellations, such as Scorpius and Orion, do look similar to what they are named after. Many of the others were named in *honor* of heroes and objects, not because of any resemblance to them. We do similar things today. The state of Washington, for example, while named after the first U.S. president, does not look like him—and it was never meant to. It is the same with the constellations.

What is a star?

The constellations are marked by stars. We think of the stars as both *tiny* and *faint* because that is how they look to us, but they are neither. They are enormous and brilliant—and they are very far away.

Stars are like our sun. Our sun is a globe of hot gas almost a million miles across—so big that if the earth were the size of a Ping-Pong ball, the sun would be the size of your bedroom. If the sun were hollow, you would need over one million earths to fill it. The sun is certainly big compared to anything else we know, but it is just an average-sized star. The stars look tiny only because they are so very distant.

Like people, each star is different. Some stars are many times the size and brightness of our sun, but others are much smaller. If we put a giant star like Deneb, from the constellation Cygnus, next to our sun, it would outshine the sun by 10,000 times. Sirius, from the constellation Canis Major, outshines our sun by 23 times. The truly faintest stars are less than a thousandth as bright as our sun, but these stars are all so dim that we cannot see any without a telescope.

Astronomers express distances to stars with *light-years.* A light-year is a unit of *distance,* not a unit of *time.* It is the distance that a beam of light travels in one year. Light travels at the enormous speed of 186,300 miles per second—fast enough to travel seven times around the earth or almost from the earth to the moon in only one second! A beam of light travels to the earth from the sun or a nearby planet in a few minutes. In one year light travels almost 6 trillion miles—approximately 65,000 times the distance from the earth to the sun.

The closest star we see from northern North America is Sirius, which is a little over 8 light-years (50 trillion miles) distant. The stars of the Big Dipper are all about 100 light-years away. The most distant bright star you can see is Deneb, which is 1,600 light-years away. The most distant object you can see without a telescope is the Andromeda Galaxy, which is over 2 *million* light-years away.

If our sun were light-*years* away instead of light *minutes,* it, too, would appear as faint as the stars in the night sky. Because it takes time for light to travel, we see a star as it was long ago, when its light began its journey to earth. We see *old* starlight.

How often do the constellations move?

The constellations are *always* in motion!

As you sit and read, the earth is carrying you and this book in two directions at once. The earth is constantly spinning and makes one complete rotation every 24 hours. It makes a complete trip around the sun once a year. Although we do not feel these motions, we see the result of them in the sky. The spin of the earth gives us night and day, while the rotation around the sun gives us our different seasons. Both of these movements cause you to see different constellations throughout the night and at different times of the year.

As the earth spins toward the east, carrying you along with it, the sky seems to turn toward the west. We say that the stars rise in the east and set in the west, although we know that it is the earth that is turning. This causes us to face different parts of the sky at different times of the night. If you watch the sky for several hours, you will see that stars (as well as the planets, the sun, and the moon) rise in the east, travel westward across the sky, and eventually set in the west. Stars that are in the east early in the evening are in the west late at night. You can see this nightly motion on your Rotating Star Finder by slowly turning the wheel in a counterclockwise direction (in the opposite way the hands move on the face of a clock). When you rotate the Star Finder, you are rotating the earth.

At the same time, the earth is orbiting around the sun. The stars we see at night lie in the opposite direction as the sun. (When stars lie in the same direction as the sun, they are in the daytime sky and we cannot see them.) As the earth moves around the sun, the part of the sky that lies opposite the sun changes month by month. The constellations we see at night change with the seasons.

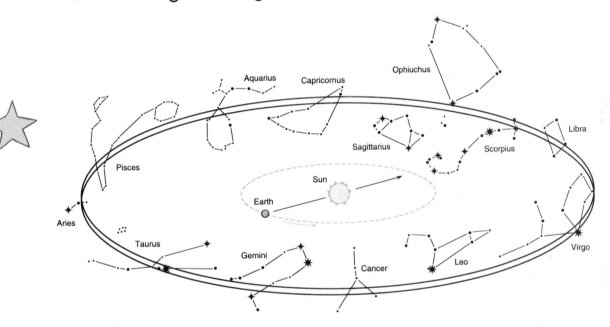

As the earth orbits the sun, the direction we face at night changes month by month. We cannot see the constellations that lie behind the sun. When the sun is in front of Taurus, for example, we see Scorpius at night. But six months later, when the earth has moved so that the sun is now in front of Scorpius, we see Taurus at night.

As the earth orbits the sun, it looks like the sun moves around the sky. The part of the sky that is hidden by the sun changes month by month. For example, the sun is in front of the stars of Taurus in summer, and we cannot see Taurus then. Six months later, in winter, the sun has moved halfway around the sky and now lies in the direction of Scorpius. Because Taurus is opposite the sun, we can see it in the night sky. We call Taurus a winter constellation because it is visible in the winter. As the earth moves around the sun, the part of the sky that is blocked by the sun changes. Constellations become invisible behind the sun, only to reappear again a few months later. Remember: The earth's orbital motion causes us to see different constellations throughout the year.

Your Rotating Star Finder will show the yearly motion of the earth. You can even plot the position of the sun on the finder—just follow the directions on pages 13 through 15.

IT'S ALL GREEK TO ME!

The brightest stars in a constellation are named with letters of the Greek alphabet. The first five letters in order are alpha (α), beta (β), gamma (γ), delta (δ), and epsilon (ε). Usually the brightest star in a constellation is named alpha. For example, Vega is known as Alpha in Lyra, or Alpha Lyrae.

Who invented the constellations?

Constellations are imaginary and someone thought up each one. A few were created in modern times, but most are thousands of years old and some are even prehistoric. Discovering the origins of the constellations is scientific detective work where we piece together the few clues that we have. Even today we still know very little about the origins of many of the most famous constellations.

Many familiar constellations were invented by the Sumerians, who lived in what is now Iraq. The Sumerians were the first systematic stargazers that we know of. More than 5,000 years ago they invented the idea of dividing the sky into the familiar patterns—such as Leo, Scorpius, and Orion—that we still see today. They were trying to understand the changes in the sky that accompany the changes in the seasons, and they charted the path of the sun and planets among the stars. The Babylonians who followed them kept this information alive until it was borrowed by the Greeks. Other constellations may have come from people in the Mediterranean, but the details are lost and we may never know their histories.

By the time of the ancient Greeks—4th century B.C.—there were 48 constellations. The Greeks gave them their own stories. The Romans borrowed the Greek descriptions of these constellations and gave them their own familiar Latin names.

After the end of the Roman Empire, learning was kept alive by the Arabs, who translated and preserved Greek and Roman books. The Arabs gave most of the stars the common names we know them by today. These names are usually Arabic translations of Greek and Roman descriptions of the stars' positions. For example, the star Rigel, found in Orion, means "foot" in Arabic—which is exactly where the star is.

The remaining 40 constellations were added relatively recently. When European navigators sailed far south of the equator, they saw for the first time stars that until then had been hidden below their southern horizon. Several new constellations, such as the Southern Triangle, were created in the early 1500s.

The German astronomer Johann Bayer is credited with adding 12 new constellations, such as the Peacock and Flying Fish, in 1603. He used reports and charts brought to him by Dutch sailors, but he did not personally see these stars.

Almost a century later seven additional constellations were invented by the Polish astronomer Johannes Hevelius, who used them to fill in places on his star atlas that looked too empty. He did this to make his charts more attractive and to "use up" faint stars that were between major constellations. These new northern constellations, such as the Lizard and the Fox, are made of faint stars and are not easy to see.

Nicolas Louis de Lacaille, a French astronomer who lived in Cape Town, South Africa, from 1750–1752, created 14 new constellations and named them after inventions and tools he thought important. Among these are the Telescope and Microscope, Air Pump, and Compass. These constellations are faint, too. Although they cannot be seen from North America or Europe, the southern constellations are briefly described in this book. Through the centuries other astronomers and map makers added new star figures to their charts or renamed old ones, and at one time there was a Battery, a Cat, and a Flying Squirrel in the sky. However, these constellations were not accepted by astronomers of the time and fell out of use. You see them only on antique star charts. The modern constellations were finalized by a committee in 1928 and will not change again.

The 88 official constellations are called western because they are part of the heritage of our western civilization. Other people in other lands divided the sky their own way and saw entirely different groups of stars. The ancient Chinese, for example, divided the sky into about 300 small constellations of only several stars each, and the ancient Egyptians saw crocodiles and hippopotamuses. Generally people dropped their own constellations when they came in contact with westerners. Today the western constellations are recognized around the world and are truly universal.

CHAPTER 2

HOW TO USE THIS BOOK

This book has all you need to teach yourself the constellations. It has directions for seeing and learning about each constellation, detailed star charts, and a Rotating Star Finder, which includes the major constellations visible from North America.

To get the most out of this handy guide, follow the steps below:

1. Have you read the Introduction and Chapter 1? These sections will give you a good basis on stargazing and its history. Now you're ready to explore the constellations in Chapter 3, from pages 18 to 66. This chapter can be read in any order and you can skip around as you wish.

2. When you find a constellation or two that you want to locate in the sky, turn to the star charts corresponding with those constellations. The charts give you a detailed look at the constellations and any surrounding nebulae, star clusters, or important stars.

3. Now pull out your Rotating Star Finder! This Star Finder shows you the entire sky as it appears at any moment on any date. You will use it to know where in the sky to look for your chosen constellations.

Unlike a regular map, which you hold in front of you, the Rotating Star Finder is used upside down! Hold it over your head. After all, that is where the sky is!

To find when a particular star or constellation will rise, locate it on your Star Finder. Then rotate the Finder's dial to put that object exactly on the eastern horizon. Find today's date on the outer rotating dial, and see what time that corresponds to. That is when the object rises. Likewise, you can determine when a constellation will set by putting it on the western horizon.

To set your Star Finder to see what the sky will look like on any given night at any hour, follow these simple steps:

A. Set the current date and time. Find the present time on the part of the finder that does not turn. The evening hours are at the upper right part of it. Be sure to pick standard or daylight time, depending on which is in use. It is okay to estimate the time. Turn the rotating dial so that today's date is next to the present time.

B. Find south and face that direction. Many city streets are aligned north-south. (If you don't know which way is south, and an adult can't help, remember that the sun sets in the west. If you know your way around the sky already, you know that the North Star is always in the north and that the opposite direction is south.)

C. Hold the Rotating Star Finder over your head. The horizon is the edge of the window, and it goes entirely around you. The paper clip or small piece of wire is the North Star, and it is behind you and partway up the northern sky. The part of the sky that is straight overhead is at the center of the window. Which constellations are visible? (You can then work backward and look up the constellations in Chapter 3 to find out more about them!)

You can also see how the sky changes as the earth turns and the hours pass. Rotate the Star Finder counterclockwise so that today's date moves to later and later hours. You can watch the stars rise in the east and set in the west.

Of course, you can set your Rotating Star Finder to *any* date and *any* time and view the sky of the past or future. You can even see where the stars are during the daytime.

Do you want to plot the position of the sun? The sun's path is the thin line that runs around the sky. That line is called the ecliptic, and the sun is always somewhere on it and within one of the 13 constellations of the astronomical zodiac, which means "ring of animals." (There are 12 "signs" in the astrological zodiac, but the signs do not correspond to the astronomical constellations and are not recognized by scientists.) Draw an imaginary straight line from today's

EAST SOUTH WEST

Face south and hold your Rotating Star Finder over your head. Check that the S is in the south, W is to the right, E is to the left, and N is behind you. The paper clip or small piece of wire is the North Star, and it is the point around which the sky pivots as the hours pass. The top of the sky is at the center of the cut-out window. The edge of the window is the horizon. Set the date and time.

date to the North Star, and the sun is where that line crosses the ecliptic. Try this during the daytime—is the sun in the correct part of the sky?

The planets move through the constellations, too, and if you discover a bright "star" in the sky that is not on your charts or Rotating Star Finder, it is a planet. The planets move around the sun so slowly that they remain for weeks or months in one constellation before moving on to the next.

Each planet is different. Mercury remains so close to the sun that you will not see it without making a special effort. Venus outshines every star, and it is often in either the west in the evening sky or in the east in the morning sky, where we call it the evening star or morning star. Mars is as bright as the brightest stars when it is near the earth, but generally it does not stand out. Jupiter is brilliant. Saturn resembles a bright star. Uranus, Neptune, and Pluto are visible only with telescopes.

The sun, moon, and planets travel through a narrow band in the sky. Usually they appear in the 13 constellations of the astronomical zodiac, but they can occasionally appear in a dozen others, too.

How should I observe the constellations?

It might sound silly to ask how to observe the constellations. Don't you just go outside at night and look up?

There's a bit more to it than that. First, it is far better to observe from a dark place. You will see *many* more stars if the sky is dark. If the sky is brightly lit, you will not see the fainter constellations or the lesser stars within any constellation. If you live in a city, there's not much you can do about the millions of city lights, but you can make sure that lights around your home are turned off. The best time to observe the stars might be while on vacation, especially in national parks and other remote areas where it is amazingly dark at night.

Find a place away from trees and houses. The most interesting part of the sky is near the southern horizon, because that is the part of the sky that changes the most as the sky turns overhead.

Needless to say, if you're not dressed comfortably, you won't enjoy sky gazing. Experienced sky watchers remember to dress warmly. Your body generates less heat to warm you if you're standing around stargazing than if you were moving around and playing. If you will be observing for a long period of time, you may want to stretch out in a lounge chair or on a pad on the ground.

Your eyes need time to adjust to the darkness. When you step outside from a brightly lit room, you won't see much at first. Allow five or more minutes for your eyes to develop "night vision," and for you to be able to see faint stars and the Milky Way. Then avoid bright lights while you observe.

Bring this book, your Rotating Star Finder, and a flashlight. Red light does not affect your night vision as much as white light, so put a piece of red cellophane over the lens of a small flashlight and read by a dim red light.

The best way to see the constellations is with your own

eyes! With your eyes alone you can see wide areas of the sky. You can see several constellations at once and you can see how they fit together and relate to each other.

To see fainter stars as well as the major "deep space" objects such as star clusters and nebulae (clouds of gas), the best instrument for constellation-watching is a pair of binoculars. They are also great for exploring the Milky Way. The best astronomy binoculars are labeled 7 X 50. Such binoculars are 7 power with a lens diameter of 50 millimeters. Smaller binoculars, such as 7 X 35 or 6 X 24, have a smaller lens and do not gather enough light from faint stars. Larger or higher-powered binoculars are expensive and need a tripod. Even if you own a huge telescope one day, you will always enjoy using binoculars.

As your interest grows, you will eventually want a telescope. Surprisingly you will *not* see the constellations better with a telescope. A telescope is great for looking at the moon, planets, and deep space objects, but a telescope shows only a tiny part of the sky at a time and is useless for viewing constellations. A flimsy and poorly made telescope is frustrating to use and may not work well. Choosing a telescope is an important decision, and one you should not make too quickly. Ask experts at planetariums and in astronomy clubs for advice.

An essential tool for your telescope is a detailed star chart to find faint objects among the stars. Again, seek advice from people in planetariums and astronomy clubs.

CHAPTER 3

THE CONSTELLATIONS
(appearing alphabetically)

Here you will find a discussion of all 88 constellations in the sky. You'll find out what time of year each appears and whether or not you can see it from where you live. Once you come across a constellation you want to see in the night sky, go to the corresponding star chart to see what it looks like. Then find it on your Rotating Star Finder! (For step-by-step instructions on using the Finder, see pages 13 through 15.)

Andromeda the Chained Maiden (see Star Chart 4, page 68)

Andromeda (an-DRAHM-uh-duh) is a major constellation in the eastern sky in the early evening during the autumn. It is a line of three equally spaced bright stars and some fainter stars to the west. The southernmost bright star of Andromeda is used to form the Great Square of Pegasus. This star, called Alpheraty, was once considered a part of Pegasus, but as no star can be in two constellations, it was officially placed in Andromeda.

Andromeda is famous for housing the Andromeda Galaxy, the large galaxy nearest to our own Milky Way.

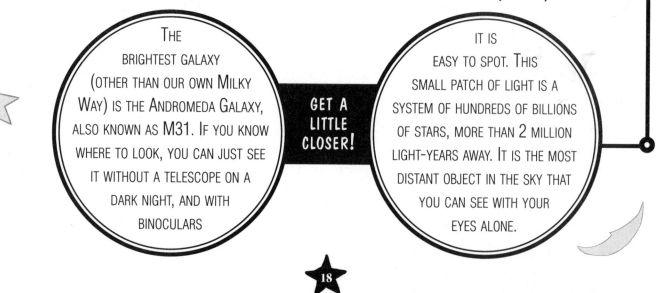

THE BRIGHTEST GALAXY (OTHER THAN OUR OWN MILKY WAY) IS THE ANDROMEDA GALAXY, ALSO KNOWN AS M31. IF YOU KNOW WHERE TO LOOK, YOU CAN JUST SEE IT WITHOUT A TELESCOPE ON A DARK NIGHT, AND WITH BINOCULARS

GET A LITTLE CLOSER!

IT IS EASY TO SPOT. THIS SMALL PATCH OF LIGHT IS A SYSTEM OF HUNDREDS OF BILLIONS OF STARS, MORE THAN 2 MILLION LIGHT-YEARS AWAY. IT IS THE MOST DISTANT OBJECT IN THE SKY THAT YOU CAN SEE WITH YOUR EYES ALONE.

PERILS OF THE PRINCESS

According to Greek mythology, Queen Cassiopeia was a vain woman who boasted she was more beautiful than even the sea nymphs. This angered Neptune, god of the sea, who sent the sea monster Cetus to ravage her kingdom as punishment. Neptune decreed that Cassiopeia's daughter, the Princess Andromeda, be chained to the rocks by the sea, where Cetus would devour her. Poor Andromeda was chained and left to her fate. As Cetus approached the Chained Maiden, the young hero Perseus arrived. He carried with him the head of Medusa—a head so ugly that it turned anyone who gazed upon it to stone. Perseus showed the head to Cetus, who turned to stone and sank into the sea. Having saved the fair princess, Perseus was given Andromeda's hand in marriage, and they flew away on the winged horse Pegasus. (If this sounds familiar, it might be because this scene appeared in the 1981 movie *Clash of the Titans.*)

Antlia the Air Pump (see Star Charts 12, page 72 & 17, page 75)

Antlia (ANT-lee-uh) is too far south to be visible from the United States. It is hardly visible at all, as it consists of only very faint stars. The French astronomer Lacaille created it in the 18th century, when an air pump was a remarkable new invention.

Apus the Bird of Paradise (see Star Chart 18, page 75)

Apus (AY-pus), a colorful tropical bird, is too far south to be seen from the United States. It first appeared on astronomer Johann Bayer's star atlas in 1603.

Aquarius the Water Carrier
(see Star Charts 10, page 71 & 15, page 74)

Before indoor plumbing, water was delivered door to door by water carriers like **Aquarius (uh-KWARE-ee-us).** On antique star charts, Aquarius is shown as a man on his knees pouring from a jug of water. In the sky, Aquarius is a large but shapeless group of faint stars that lies south and west of Pegasus.

Aquarius seems to be associated with the "great flood" that we are told once inundated the entire world—a story that had its origin in Sumeria and that later appeared in the Old Testament of the Bible, among other places.

You can see Aquarius in the southern sky from August through October.

Aquila the Eagle (see Star Chart 15, page 74)

The Eagle lies in the Milky Way. We see it best during the summer. In Greek mythology, **Aquila (uh-KWEE-luh)** carried the thunderbolts of Zeus, the king of the gods.

Aquila's brightest star is Altair— the southernmost star of the trio of three bright stars we call the Summer Triangle (see page 47). The other two stars of the Summer Triangle are Vega in

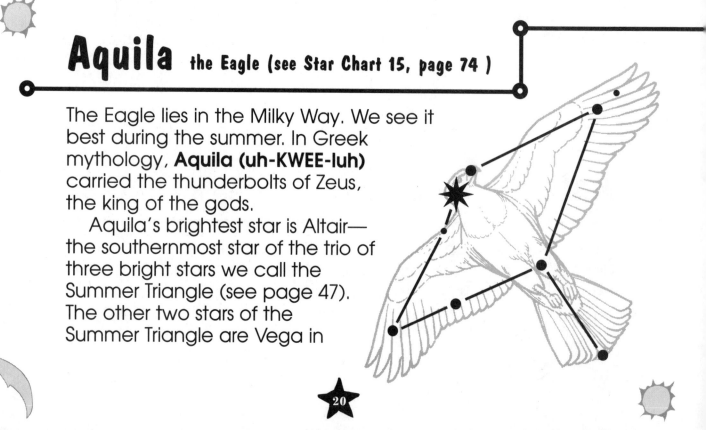

THE ZODIAC

The zodiac is a band of constellations that the sun travels through in its annual trip around the sky. As the earth travels around the sun once a year, it looks like the sun travels around the sky. The sun travels through 13 constellations (not just the 12 most people think of), and these are the constellations of the zodiac. The moon and planets also stay within this band most of the time. The constellations of the zodiac are well known because the sun, moon, and planets travel through them, but many of them are minor constellations that contain no bright stars.

Have you heard the song "The Age of Aquarius"? Well, the true Age of Aquarius will begin in about 600 years, when, for the first time, the sun will be in Aquarius on the first day of spring.

To see Aquila as an eagle in flight with outstretched wings:

1. Imagine that Altair is the Eagle's head.

2. One wing stretches up to the stars in the north and the other stretches down to stars in the south.

3. The tail extends away from the head to the southwest.

Lyra and Deneb in Cygnus. Altair looks similar to Deneb in brightness, but Deneb is 100 times more distant and 10,000 times more luminous, proving that you cannot tell much about a star just by looking at it.

It is tricky the first time you try to make an eagle of these stars.

Ara the Altar (see Star Charts 16, page 74 & 18, page 75)

Ara (AIR-uh) represents an altar used for sacrifices. It is a small and faint constellation. From the northern United States it never rises high enough to see, and from the southern states it rises only a short distance above the southern horizon, and then just briefly. Look for it below the tail of Scorpius the Scorpion at about 10:00 P.M. in July. Ara looks like two parallel strings of faint stars.

Aries the Ram (see Star Charts 4, page 68 & 5, page 69)

Aries (AIR-eez) is a large constellation with only three medium-bright stars in its northern part. These three stars form a simple pattern that is easy to recognize, but—despite its fame as a member of the zodiac—the constellation is not very interesting to observe. Aries is in the east in the autumn and high overhead in late December and January.

In Sumerian times these stars were a "day laborer" who plowed a field to plant grain. It has been called a ram since at least the time of the ancient Greeks.

Four thousand years ago the earth was oriented so that the sun was in Aries on the first day of spring (March 22), a day that then was considered the first day of the year. At that time the sun's position was called the "first point of Aries." The sun is now in Pisces on the first day of spring, but Aries is still called the first constellation of the zodiac in memory of this ancient alignment. When any planet is "visiting" Aries, the planet is brighter than any of the constellation's stars.

Auriga the Charioteer
(see Star Charts 5 & 6, page 69)

Auriga (aw-REE-guh) is a large ring of many bright stars. The brightest star is Capella. The star in the ring farthest from Capella is actually in the constellation Taurus (it is Beta). Beta is needed to complete Auriga's ring.

Because this large constellation is so

STAR SEARCH

Auriga's brightest star is Capella (kuh-PEH-luh), a yellow giant star that is the sixth brightest star in the sky and the northernmost bright star. It is 45 light-years from earth. Capella is midway between Orion and the North Star. *Capella* means "the little she-goat."

far to the north, Auriga is visible most of the night most of the year. It is straight overhead in January and February but not visible on summer evenings.

In Greek mythology Auriga was a chariot driver or charioteer, but he is shown without the chariot. On old star charts he is holding one goat (the star Capella) over his shoulder and a group of young goats, called the Kids, in his arms. He may originally have been seen as a shepherd.

The Milky Way runs through Auriga.

Boötes the Herdsman

(see Star Charts 7 & 8, page 70)

Boötes (boh-OH-teez) is nearly overhead during the early evening in late spring and early summer.

Boötes is shaped like a kite. To find it:

1. Start with the Big Dipper. Find the five stars in the Dipper's handle. They form an arc, like the arc of a wheel.

2. Continue the arc about a dipper's length to the south to the star Arcturus. Think of: "arc to Arcturus."

3. Arcturus is the southernmost star in this kite-shaped figure that extends to the north and east. Two other stars are a short distance east and west of Arcturus.

STAR SEARCH

Arktos (ARK-tohs) is Greek for "bear," and *Arcturus* (ark-TOOR-us) means "bear watcher," and it appears to chase the Great Bear around the pole. It is the second brightest star visible from most of the United States. Arcturus is a giant orange-yellow star, 20 times the diameter and 110 times as bright as our sun. Compare its color with other bright stars (Vega to the east is blue-white and Spica to the south is white). At a distance of only 36 light-years, it is the closest giant star to earth.

23

You can think of Boötes as an ice-cream cone with Arcturus at the bottom.

Because Boötes follows the Great Bear around the sky, he is called the bear driver or the bear herder. In England, where the bear is seen as a plow, Boötes is called the plowman.

Caelum the Chisel (see Star Charts 16, page 74 & 17, page 75)

Caelum (SEE-lum) is one of the smallest constellations. It is made of very faint stars. It lies south of Orion and barely rises above the horizon as seen from the United States.

Caelum, a sculptor's engraving chisel, was created by the astronomer Lacaille in the 1750s and has no mythology tied to it.

Camelopardalis the Giraffe
(see Star Charts 1 & 2, page 67)

The Giraffe is a scraggly string of faint stars that occupies a basically empty area of the sky between the North Star and Perseus. It is high overhead in the winter.

To the Greeks a **camelopardalis (kuh-meh-luh-PAHR-duh-luss)** was a creature with the body of a giraffe, the head of a camel, and the spots of a leopard. The constellation itself, however, is not Greek. It was invented by the Dutch map maker Plancius in 1613, who named it after the Greek mythological creature.

Cancer the Crab (see Star Chart 6, page 69)

Cancer (KAN-sir) is one of the faintest constellations of the zodiac. If it weren't for its membership in the zodiac, few people would have heard of it. It has no bright stars.

Cancer is midway between the major constellations Leo and Gemini. It is in the early evening sky from February through May.

In Greek mythology Cancer was a crab that was sent to bite Hercules. Hercules squashed it easily. Ancient Egyptians saw it as a scarab beetle, the Babylonians may have seen it as a turtle, and on some old star maps it was a lobster.

Canes Venatici the Hunting Dogs

(see Star Charts 3, page 68; 7 & 8, page 70)

There are three dog constellations: the Great Dog, the Small Dog, and the Hunting Dogs, called **Canes Venatici (KAY-nuss vay-NUH-tih-see).** The Great and Small Dogs are prominent ancient constellations, but the Hunting Dogs are faint and were created only in 1690, by Johannes Hevelius. They are the Hunting Dogs of nearby Boötes, and they accompany him as they follow the Great Bear around the pole of the sky.

The Hunting Dogs are immediately south of the Big Dipper's handle, and they are visible at the same time as the Dipper (best in spring and early summer, but they can

STAR SEARCH

Although Cancer has no bright stars, it has one of the brightest star clusters. The Beehive (also known as M44) is smack in the middle of Cancer. On the darkest nights the Beehive is barely visible without binoculars. With binoculars it looks like a little fuzzy patch of light. A small telescope will show several dozen faint stars. The Beehive is 520 light-years away.

GET A LITTLE CLOSER!

THE FIRST GALAXY WHOSE SPIRAL SHAPE WAS SEEN THROUGH A TELESCOPE IS M51, FOUND IN CANES VENATICI. IT IS VISIBLE IN A GOOD AMATEUR TELESCOPE, BUT ONLY A VERY LARGE TELESCOPE WILL SHOW ITS SPIRAL STRUCTURE. M51 IS A SHORT DISTANCE SOUTHWEST OF ALKAID, THE END STAR IN THE HANDLE OF THE BIG DIPPER. M51 IS ABOUT 20 MILLION LIGHT-YEARS FROM EARTH.

be viewed year-round). The only star that is even medium bright is Cor Caroli (Latin for "the Heart of Charles," in honor of England's King Charles I). Cor Caroli (kor kuh-ROH-lee) is at the center of the arc formed by the five stars in the handle and bowl of the Big Dipper.

Canis Major the Large Dog (see Star Chart 12, page 72)

STAR SEARCH

Sirius (SEAR-ee-us), also called the Dog Star, is the brightest star in the sky. It is also the closest star visible from the United States (at only 8.6 light-years distant). It is twice the diameter and 23 times as bright as our sun. Its name means "scorcher" in Greek. It is brilliant white with a touch of blue. When it is near the horizon, it can twinkle wildly and flash with all the colors of the rainbow.

When the ancient Egyptians saw Sirius rise before the sun, they knew the annual life-giving flood of the Nile River would soon follow. They thought Sirius brought life, and perhaps they thought it caused the river's flooding. The first appearance of Sirius in the summer's morning sky marked the beginning of their year (the ancient Egyptian New Year's Day).

Canis Major (KAY-nuss MAY-jer) is the largest hunting dog that accompanies the giant hunter Orion in his nightly journey across the sky. It follows Orion, rising in the southeast after his master and staying to the lower left of the giant. Because Canis Major contains Sirius, the brightest star in the sky, it is very easy to find.

Both Canis Major and Canis Minor are in the evening sky from January until May.

The Milky Way is immediately to the east of Canis Major.

To see Canis Major as a dog:

1. Find Sirius. Notice that Sirius is in line with Orion's belt of three bright stars.

2. The dog's front legs are the stars immediately to the right of Sirius.

3. Find the brightest star below Sirius. This is the dog's hindquarters. The rear legs extend from this star to the right.

4. Sirius can be the jewel in the dog's collar. Then the dog's head is the few stars to the upper left of Sirius. If you, like some people, imagine Sirius as the tip of the dog's nose, make his back a little shorter, and have his front legs extend straighter from his body.

Canis Minor the Small Dog
(see Star Charts 6, page 69 & 12, page 72)

Canis Minor (KAY-nuss MY-ner) is the small hunting dog who follows his larger doggy companion Canis Major, as well as Orion the Hunter, across the sky. It is best visible in the winter.

Canis Minor is essentially a two-star constellation. Procyon (PRO-see-on) is very bright and easy to find, while the other star, Gomeisa (go-MY-zuh), is a short distance to the northwest.

Procyon is usually the small dog's tail and Gomeisa is his head. Canis Minor is indeed "small," but it doesn't look much like a dog!

STAR SEARCH

Procyon is Greek for "before the dog," and it was given this name long ago, when it used to rise before the Dog Star Sirius. In the 20th century Procyon rises within a few minutes of Sirius, but 3,000 years ago (when the earth's axis was tilted in a different direction) Procyon rose more than half an hour before Sirius. Thousands of years from now Procyon will *follow* Sirius across the sky.

Procyon is a cosmic next-door neighbor only 11⅓ light-years distant. If you are 11 years and 4 months old, the starlight you see tonight left Procyon when you were born. The only closer bright star you can see from the United States is Sirius. Procyon is slightly yellow in color and is not as white as Sirius.

Capricornus the Sea-Goat (see Star Chart 15, page 74)

The sun, moon, and planets pass through **Capricornus (kap-rih-KORN-us)** as they travel around the sky, making it a constellation of the zodiac. Capricornus is best visible in the early autumn.

A sea-goat, also called a goat-fish, is an odd creature you will not find at the zoo. It is a goat with a fish's tail. In Sumerian times about 5,000 years ago, the Sumerians created imaginary new animals by combining familiar animals in strange ways. Sagittarius, half-man and half-horse, and Pegasus, a horse with wings, are two other examples.

Capricornus has no bright stars.

Carina the Keel (see Star Chart 17, page 75)

There used to be an enormous constellation in the southern sky called Argo the Ship. It was so huge that 19th century astronomers broke it up and divided it into Puppis the Stern, Vela the Sails, Pyxis the Nautical Compass, and **Carina (kuh-REE-nuh)** the Keel. (Pyxis was originally the Mast, but Lacaille transformed it into a compass in the 1750s.) You will see Argo on some star charts, but it is no longer an official constellation.

WHO WAS THE OWNER OF THIS GREAT SHIP?

Jason, a mythical hero of ancient times, manned the *Argo.* Kids knew him long before there ever existed heroes such as James Bond or Indiana Jones. He led the Argonauts in all sorts of adventures in their ship, the *Argo.*

The Stern, Sails, and Compass are just visible low in the southern sky in winter from much of the United States, but Carina—being the lowest part of a ship—is too far to the south to see. All of Carina that can be seen from the southernmost states is the bright star Canopus.

Cassiopeia the Queen (see Star Chart 1, page 67)

Cassiopeia (ka-see-oh-PEE-yuh) is a major winter constellation. After the Big Dipper, it is probably the best-known star pattern in the northern sky. People who can recognize only a few constellations likely know the five-star W shape of Cassiopeia.

The main part of Cassiopeia lies near the sky's north pole and is visible all night and all year. The best time to see it is when it is at its highest, during the early evening from August through February—more than half the year. Cassiopeia rises in the northeast as a letter *W* and sets in the northwest as a sideways letter *M.*

Cassiopeia sits opposite the Big Dipper with the North Star between them, so as one rises, the other sets, and when one is high, the other is low. The Big Dipper is a spring constellation and Cassiopeia is an autumn constellation.

In Greek mythology Cassiopeia is a queen seated on her throne, and she is often called the seated lady. She was a queen of Ethiopia, in Africa. Her daughter, Andromeda, is featured in Perils of the Princess on page 19. These two constellations, along with the constellation Cepheus, Cassiopeia's husband, are grouped together in the fall sky.

The Milky Way passes through Cassiopeia, and the constellation has several star clusters, visible through small telescopes.

Centaurus the Centaur (see Star Charts 17 & 18, page 75)

Centaurus (sen-TOR-us) is an ancient constellation that lies far to the south. The northern part of it can be seen from the southern part of the United States, but the lowest part of the Centaur cannot be seen from any place north of the southernmost tip of Florida and Hawaii. The top part of Centaurus is an indistinct group of faint stars below Virgo and can be found just above the southern horizon in May and June.

A centaur is a composite beast, half-man and half-horse, and known to be very rowdy. However, this Centaur, whose name was Chiron (KY-run), was kind and gentle. The other centaur in the sky is Sagittarius.

Cepheus the King (see Star Charts 1, page 67 & 3, page 68)

Cepheus (SEE-fee-us or SEE-fyoos) is a large group of dim stars, and it takes some practice to learn to see it. It lies in a basically empty part of the sky near Cassiopeia and Cygnus. The Milky Way runs nearby.

Cepheus is near the sky's north pole and it is high overhead during the autumn. However, you can see it in the evening sky from August through December.

Cepheus has the shape of a simple house.

To see Cepheus as a house (often upside down) of five stars:

1. Find Cassiopeia, the W-shaped constellation to the east.

2. Find the faint star that is halfway between the westernmost star of the W (Beta in Cassiopeia) and the North Star. This star marks the "top of the house" that is Cepheus.

3. The four corners of the house are equally spaced to the south and west, and they form a square of faint stars. The southernmost corner of this square is actually three faint stars grouped together.

In Greek mythology Cepheus was King of Ethiopia, the husband of Queen Cassiopeia and the father of Princess Andromeda.

Cetus the Whale (see Star Charts 10, page 71 & 11, page 72)

Cetus (SEE-tuss) is the fourth-largest constellation, but it has no bright stars or particular shape. It lies south of Aries and Pisces, and like them, it is in the evening sky during the autumn.

Cetus was the monster sent to devour Andromeda (see the tale under the constellation Andromeda).

Chamaeleon the Chameleon (see Star Chart 17, page 75)

The **Chamaeleon (kuh-MEE-lee-un)** is a small constellation of faint stars near the sky's south pole, and it can't be seen from the United States. Invented by Bayer in 1603, it has no mythology.

Chameleons are a type of lizard known for their ability to change color to match their background. There are two lizards in the sky. The other is Lacerta.

Circinus the Compasses (see Star Chart 18, page 75)

Circinus (SIR-suh-nuss), the Compasses, is the fourth smallest constellation. Astronomer Lacaille squeezed it between Centaurus and Triangulum Australe—another drawing tool—in his effort to fill the sky with technical tools. It has only faint stars and is too far south to be visible from the United States.

Columba the Dove (see Star Chart 17, page 75)

Far south of Orion in the winter sky is **Columba (koh-LUM-buh)** the Dove. It has only a few medium-bright stars and is hard to see.

Columba is named after the dove released by Noah to find dry land following the Biblical flood, found in the first chapter in the Bible, Genesis. It was invented by the map maker Petrus Plancius and first appeared on charts in the 1600s.

To find Columba:

1. Draw an imaginary line from Procyon (the brightest star in Canis Minor) to Sirius (the brightest star in Canis Major).

2. Continue the same distance in the same direction. That will take you to the center of the Dove. The Dove is low in the south at around 8:00 P.M. in February.

Coma Berenices Berenice's Hair

(see Star Chart 7, page 70)

This swarm of faint stars, **Coma Berenices (KOH-muh bear-uh-NEYE-seez),** lies midway between Boötes and Leo. It is high in the sky all spring and overhead in the early evening in May.

The constellation is named after a real person, and the story of how the constellation got its name is more interesting than the stars themselves. Queen Berenice was wife of King Ptolemy III of ancient Egypt. She offered to cut off her beautiful hair if her husband returned safely from a battle. When he did, she cut her hair and placed it in a shrine in a temple. One day the hair was found missing, and the king threatened revenge on the temple guards. The court astronomer saved the day by showing the angry king and queen a faint group of stars and telling them that the gods were so impressed that they had placed the queen's hair in the sky for all to see.

The stars of the constellation are actually a star cluster—a group of dozens of stars traveling together through space. It is called the Coma Star Cluster, and it is about 250 light-years away. It is so large (about the size of the bowl of the Big Dipper) that it is best seen with binoculars on a very dark night (but not with a telescope, which shows only part of it at a time). The only closer bright cluster of stars is the Hyades in the constellation Taurus, which is about half as far from earth as the Coma Star Cluster.

Corona Australis the Southern Crown
(see Star Charts 16, page 74 & 18, page 75)

Corona Australis (kuh-ROW-nuh aws-TRAY-luss) is a ring, or crown, of stars directly below Sagittarius and straight to the left of the tail of Scorpius. The stars are all faint, but the ring is so complete that it is surprisingly easy to see from the southern United States. Because the ring is so far to the south, it is difficult to see from the northern states and Canada. It is just above the southern horizon early in the evening in August.

To the Greeks this was a laurel wreath worn at times of glory. Today it is most commonly shown as a gold crown.

Corona Borealis the Northern Crown
(see Star Chart 8, page 70)

This is the second crown in the sky. It is a ring with one star that is much brighter than the others, so it looks like a diamond ring. This constellation is immediately east of Boötes and is best seen in the spring and early summer, when it is nearly overhead.

Like Corona Australis, **Corona Borealis (kuh-ROW-nuh bore-ee-AL-us)** is not a gold crown worn by kings (although it is sometimes shown this way on star maps). Like its southern companion, it is a wreath of laurel leaves worn by victors of Greek athletic events and later by the Roman emperors.

If you think of Boötes as an ice-cream cone, you can think of Corona Borealis as a scoop of ice cream that fell off it and landed nearby.

Corvus the Crow (see Star Charts 13, page 73 & 18, page 75)

Corvus (KOR-vuss) is a small constellation best visible in the spring from April through June. It rises in the southeast and sets in the southwest.

Corvus is a crow (or sometimes a raven) that was associated with the god Apollo in Greek myths.

To find Corvus:

1. Find the constellation Virgo.

2. Then find the bright star Spica in Virgo. Look to the right and below the star.

3. Corvus looks like a bent box.

Crater the Cup (see Star Charts 13, page 73 & 17, page 75)

Crater (KRAY-ter) is associated with Corvus in mythology and in the sky. This small constellation sits to the right of Corvus. Crater's stars are not as bright and its pattern is not as easy to recognize as its neighbor.

To astronomers a crater is a bowl-shaped hole in the ground that is made when a meteorite hits a planet and explodes. The moon's surface is covered with craters. A crater is also a large bowl or a cup, like the kind that is filled with punch at a party. It was used in ancient Greece and Rome for mixing wine and water. Both types of craters have a similar shape.

The celestial Crater is straight south of the tail of Leo the Lion. Look for a half-circle of stars just to the right of Corvus. The best time to see it is in the late spring, from April through June.

Crux the Southern Cross (see Star Charts 17 & 18, page 75)

Crux (KRUKS), the Southern Cross, is one of the best-known constellations. It can only be seen from the United States in Hawaii and southern Florida.

Crux was first called a cross by European navigators around 1500. At that time it was part of Centaurus. It is now the smallest constellation. In fact, it would almost fit within the bowl of the Big Dipper.

Cygnus the Swan or Northern Cross (see Star Chart 9, page 71)

To see Cygnus as a swan flying downward:

1. Imagine that the faint star Albireo (al-BEER-ee-oh) is the swan's head.

2. His neck and body extend northward to end at the star Deneb (which means "tail" in Arabic).

3. One wing stretches toward the constellation Draco and the other toward the constellation Pegasus.

4. The tail feathers are a half-ring of faint stars to either side of Deneb.

Cygnus (SIG-nuss) is a major constellation in the summer sky. It is high overhead in the early evening from July through September. Its brightest star is Deneb.

The constellation has two popular names. In ancient times it was the Swan, but for the last few centuries it has also been called the Northern Cross. It can look like either, depending on your preference.

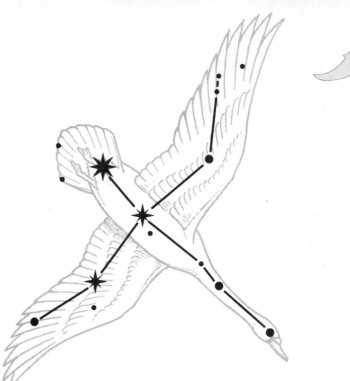

STAR SEARCH

Deneb (DEN-ebb) is one of the three stars of the Summer Triangle. It looks bright because it is! It outshines our sun by over 50,000 times and is a giant star. However, it is far, far away. Even at the enormous distance of 1,600 light-years from earth, it still looks bright. If it were as close as many other bright stars we see, it would outshine all the stars of the sky. Deneb is the most distant bright star. The light we see from Deneb began traveling to the earth around the year 400 A.D., toward the end of the Roman Empire.

The Northern Cross is several times the size of Crux, the Southern Cross. At 8:00 P.M. at Christmastime the Cross stands upright on the northwest horizon.

In Greek mythology the Swan was originally a young boy, Phaeton, who was changed into a swan by the god Zeus.

Albireo (also called Beta) is two stars close together, one blue and one yellow, as seen through a small telescope.

Cygnus lies in the Milky Way and contains within its boundaries several star clusters and nebulae that are visible through amateur telescopes.

Delphinus the Dolphin

(see Star Charts 9, page 71 & 15, page 74)

Delphinus (del-FEYE-nuss) is one of the smallest constellations that is easy to identify, and with a bit of imagination it resembles a cute little dolphin leaping out of the water. It also looks like a small kite with a tail. It has no bright stars, but you can see over a dozen faint stars within the constellation on a dark night.

The Dolphin is straight south of Cygnus and east of Aquila, and it is best seen in the summer.

Dolphins were familiar creatures to Greek and Phoenician sailors, who placed this constellation in the sky.

Dorado the Swordfish (see Star Charts 16, page 74 & 17, page 75)

The Swordfish is a string of faint stars near the sky's south pole, far south of Orion. It is not visible from the United States.

Dorado **(doh-RAH-doh)** means "golden" in Spanish, and the constellation is sometimes called Goldfish. This is not the kind of small orange fish you might keep as a pet in a bowl, but a large tasty fish related to the mahimahi popular in seafood restaurants.

The Swordfish first appeared on Bayer's atlas in 1603, and, being modern, there is no mythology associated with it.

Draco the Dragon (see Star Chart 3, page 68)

The Dragon is a huge constellation of faint stars that winds between the Big and Little Dippers, curves around the Little Dipper, and then bends back to end near the bright star Vega. It is not hard to see once you know where to look.

Draco (DRAY-koh) can always be seen from the northern United States and Canada, but it is best observed in summer, when it is highest. Look for it high in the north at 9:00 P.M. in early August.

Don't confuse the head of the Dragon with a similar small

group of stars in Hercules, which is nearby.

In ancient mythology dragons often guarded treasures. This dragon guards the sky's north pole.

To the ancient Egyptians these stars formed a hippopotamus.

STAR SEARCH

The faint star Thuban, found in Draco, is labeled on the star chart. Believe it or not, it was the North Star about 5,000 years ago!

To find Draco:

1. Find the Big and Little Dippers. (The North Star is the end of the handle of the Little Dipper.)

2. Go a little more than a third of the way from the North Star to the star at the end of the Big Dipper's bowl; you have come to the end of Draco's tail.

3. The Dragon's body curves all the way around the bowl of the Little Dipper. It bends sharply at a point about halfway between the North Star and the bright star Vega.

4. The neck of the Dragon extends southward toward a point just west of Vega.

5. The neck ends in Draco's head, which is a compact group of four stars about one-third of the way between Vega and the bowl of the Little Dipper.

Equuleus

the Little Horse or Colt
(see Star Charts 4, page 68; 9, page 71; & 15, page 74)

Equuleus (ee-KWOO-lee-us) is a tiny constellation that has only a few very faint stars. You'll find it between Pegasus and Aquila in the early autumn sky.

Recognized as long ago as the second century B.C., this little colt is a companion to Pegasus, the much larger horse nearby.

Eridanus the River (see Star Charts 11, page 72 & 16, page 74)

Eridanus (eh-RID-uh-nuss) is the second longest constellation in the sky. It winds, like a river, as a long string of stars from

To find Eridanus:

1. Find Rigel, a bright star in Orion. The River begins with a faint star a short distance to the upper right of Rigel.

2. The River is a long loop of faint stars that extends down and to the right.

3. It then bends around almost the same distance.

4. The River bends back to the west and extends far to the south, below the horizon, ending in the bright star Achernar. This is the ninth brightest star in the sky, but it is not visible from the United States north of Miami, Florida, or Hawaii. Achernar is Arabic for "end of the river."

near Orion far to the south. With the exception of its southernmost star, *Achernar* (AY-ker-nar), it is made of only faint stars, and it takes some practice to see it. The southernmost part of it is below the horizon for people in the United States. The rest of it is in the evening sky in winter.

Eridanus is an ancient constellation that was associated with the Nile River in Egypt.

Fornax the Furnace (see Star Charts 11, page 72 & 16, page 74)

Fornax (FOR-naks), a small constellation, was created by Lacaille. He thought of it as a furnace for the use of the Sculptor, another constellation he created at the same time. It is made of a few faint stars that lie within a bend in the constellation Eridanus. It is low in the southern sky in December and January.

Gemini the Twins (see Star Chart 6, page 69)

The winter sky is full of bright stars. Two that are equal in brightness and close together have been known as the "twin stars" for thousands of years. They are the heads of

Gemini (JEM-uh-neye), twin brothers Castor (KASS-tor) and Pollux (POL-uks) in Greek mythology. Gemini is a constellation of the zodiac.

Gemini is overhead in winter and early spring. In the middle of May the Twins stand upright on the northwest horizon around 8:00 P.M.

Gemini looks like two boys standing (or lying) side by side. It is two strings of stars stretching westward from the bright stars Castor and Pollux. To remember which is which, Castor is nearest to Capella (the brightest star in Auriga), and Pollux is next to Procyon (the brightest star in Canis Minor).

In Greek mythology these heroic twins were best known for their travels with Jason. Castor was an expert horseman, his twin, Pollux, an expert boxer, and together they had lots of fun battling bad guys. Because they rose before the sun as winter storms ended and as the sailing season resumed, they were popular with Greek sailors, who also looked to them for protection from pirates.

Grus the Crane (see Star Chart 16, page 74)

The Crane is a southern constellation. It can be observed just above the southern horizon in the middle of autumn.

Grus (GRUHSS), the Crane, is a water bird with a long neck, long legs, and a long bill. It first appeared on Bayer's star atlas in 1603.

Hercules the Strong Man (see Star Chart 8, page 70)

The Strong Man passes overhead in the summer. He has no very bright stars, but the two bright stars Vega and Arcturus guide you to him.

Today we call **Hercules (HER-cue-leez)** the Strong Man, but before Greek and Roman times he was the Kneeler—a man on bended knee. What the Kneeler was supposed to do was forgotten by the time of the ancient Greeks, but he may have been the Sumerian god of war. To us, Hercules is an ancient "Superman" whose strength was beyond that of normal men. In Greek mythology the first labor of Hercules was to slay a lion (Leo), who was unaffected by ordinary weapons. Hercules ended up strangling it with his bare hands, a feat also performed in the Old Testament of the Bible by Samson.

If you have a really good imagination, you can also see Hercules as the letter *H* or as a butterfly (try it yourself).

GET A LITTLE CLOSER!

AMATEUR ASTRONOMERS WITH GOOD TELESCOPES ENJOY LOOKING AT THE CLUSTER OF STARS KNOWN AS M13. THIS GROUP OF SEVERAL HUNDRED THOUSAND STARS LOOKS LIKE A SPHERE OR GLOBE, AND IT IS THE BRIGHTEST "GLOBULAR" CLUSTER IN THE NORTHERN SKY. THROUGH SMALL TELESCOPES IT LOOKS LIKE A FUZZY ROUND PATCH OF LIGHT, BUT WITH A TELESCOPE AT LEAST SIX INCHES IN DIAMETER YOU CAN BEGIN TO SEE INDIVIDUAL FAINT STARS. IT IS ABOUT 25,000 LIGHT-YEARS DISTANT. LOOK FOR M13 A THIRD OF THE WAY BETWEEN THE TWO WESTERNMOST STARS OF THE KEYSTONE.

Horologium the Clock
(see Star Charts 16, page 74 & 17, page 75)

Horologium (hor-uh-LOW-jee-um) is a string of stars lying far to the south in the winter sky. Only the top part of it is above the horizon as seen from the United States, but its stars are so faint that in reality you probably will not see it at all. It looks nothing like a clock, and there is no mythology associated with it.

This is another mechanical invention that Lacaille immortalized in the sky. He gave it the unwieldy name Horologium Oscillatorium—the Pendulum Clock—now shortened to just Horologium (not much of an improvement!).

Hydra the female Water Snake
(see Star Charts 12, page 72 & 13, page 73)

We seldom see water snakes, but there are two in the sky: **Hydra (HI-druh),** the female, and Hydrus, the male. Hydra is an ancient constellation from Sumerian times, but Hydrus first appeared on Bayer's star chart of 1603.

Hydra appears in the south in the spring. It is the largest constellation, as it zigzags across one quarter of the sky. Its stars are so faint and so far apart that it doesn't look much like a snake—or like anything else. Hydra's head is immediately below Cancer, her body winds below Leo and Crater (which touches her back) and Corvus (which "sits" on her), then under Virgo. It is so long that her head is setting when her tail is rising.

Her brightest star is Alphard (AL-fard), which means "solitary one" in Arabic—a good name for such a lonely star, which sits in the sky with no bright stars near it. Alphard is below and west of Regulus in Leo.

In mythology Hydra was a many-headed snake killed by Hercules.

Hydrus the male Water Snake (see Star Chart 16, page 74)

This constellation is a triangle of stars near the sky's south pole. It is easy to see from South America, Africa, and Australia, but it is too far south to be seen from the United States.

Hydrus (HI-druss) is a modern constellation that first appeared in Bayer's star atlas, and it is not tied to any mythology.

Indus the American Indian
(see Star Charts 16, page 74 & 18, page 75)

America was a new and almost unexplored land when Bayer included **Indus (IN-duss),** the American Indian, on his famous star atlas in 1603.

Indus lies far to the south, below Capricornus, in the autumn sky. It is a small group of faint stars with no particular shape and thus is virtually impossible to see from the United States. We would be able to see its northernmost stars from the southern United States if those stars were brighter.

Lacerta the Lizard
(see Star Charts 1, page 67; 4, page 68; & 9, page 71)

Lacerta (luh-SIR-tuh) has no bright stars, and although it passes high overhead in the autumn, it is very difficult to see its stars. Hevelius, the Polish astronomer who created it, said he put a lizard there because "nothing else would fit."

Lacerta is straight south of Cepheus and north of Pegasus. The Lizard lies in the Milky Way and has plenty of faint stars within its boundaries.

Leo the Lion

(see Star Chart 7, page 70)

Leo (LEE-oh) is a major constellation that is best seen in the springtime. The first appearance of Leo in the evening sky in March announces that spring is coming, and the Lion remains in the evening sky through June. It is one of the few constellations that can be made to look like what it is named after. *Leo* is Latin for "lion" and is one of the zodiacal constellations. *Regulus* (REG-yoo-luss), Leo's brightest star, is Latin for "Little King."

Few of us see lions today except at the zoo, but to ancient Sumerians 5,000 years ago, lions were familiar predators who ventured down to the river valleys during hot summer days and hunted sheep and goats. These stars have been seen as a lion since those prehistoric days.

To see Leo as a lion:

1. Look for a backward question mark with the bright star Regulus at the bottom of the question mark.

2. Then look for a smaller right triangle of stars to the east. The triangle is the lion's tail, his head is the circular part of the question mark, his chest is the straight part of the question mark, and his body stretches between his head and tail.

3. The star Regulus is the lion's heart, and the lion is lying on his stomach, facing Cancer to the west. The backward question mark is an easily recognizable group of stars called the Sickle, after the primitive harvesting tool that has the same shape as the star pattern.

Leo Minor the Small Lion
(see Star Charts 6, page 69 & 7, page 70)

The Small Lion lies north of Leo—the "big" Lion—and south of Ursa Major. **Leo Minor (LEE-oh MY-ner)** is a faint constellation that is best seen in the spring. It is a string of three faint stars midway between the bowl of the Big Dipper and the star Regulus in Leo. Leo Minor was devised by Hevelius, and it first appeared on his 1690 star atlas.

Lepus the Hare or Rabbit
(see Star Charts 11, page 72 & 17, page 75)

Below the constellation Orion's feet is a rabbit hiding from the Hunter, perhaps hoping to go unnoticed while Orion hunts bigger game—the constellation Taurus the Bull. **Lepus (LEAP-us)** is often overlooked because brighter constellations are nearby, but it can easily be spotted in the sky at the same time as Orion—in the middle of winter.

Libra the Balance Scales (see Star Chart 14, page 73)

Libra (LEE-bruh) is a box of four medium-bright stars to the right of Scorpius. The box is standing on one end, resembling a diamond. It is at its best spot for viewing in the early summer, when it is in the southern sky.

Libra is a set of balance scales that work by balancing two pans hanging from a lever, like the scales of justice seen on court buildings. The Sumerians may have originally called these stars scales because the sun was in front of these stars on the first day of autumn, when day and night are *balanced* in length.

Libra is the only nonanimal in the zodiac. The stars of Libra were once seen as claws that belonged to

Scorpius to the east. If you look at the Scorpion carefully, he is missing his claws. While it may make more sense for Libra's stars to be Scorpion's claws, ancient astronomers who wanted to divide the zodiac into 12 equal parts borrowed these stars to form a separate constellation.

Lupus the Wolf (see Star Chart 18, page 75)

Lupus (LOO-puss) lies directly below Libra, and you can see it in the summer. Lupus has several bright stars, but it is hard to see because it is so low in the sky. It can't be seen from the northern United States, but from the southern states it is two connected rings of stars. Look for it below Libra and to the lower right of Antares, the bright red star in Scorpius. The top part of Lupus is level with the lower part of Scorpius, so if you can't see the Scorpion's tail, you won't see Lupus.

On old illustrated star charts the poor wolf is often shown being carried on the spear of constellation Centaurus!

Lynx the Lynx or Bobcat (see Star Charts 6, page 69 & 7, page 70)

Lynx (LINKS) is faint and uninteresting. It covers a large area of the sky north of Cancer and Gemini and between Ursa Major and Auriga in the late winter and early spring.

Lynx was named by Hevelius in 1690. He said that only a person with the eyes of a lynx could see it.

Lyra the Harp (see Star Charts 3, page 68; 8, page 70; & 9, page 71)

The Harp is a compact and easy-to-recognize pattern of one star that is very bright and five stars that are fairly bright. Vega dominates the group, which is small enough to fit within the bowl of the Big Dipper.

Lyra (LIE-ruh) is nearly overhead at the end of summer and beginning of fall.

Lyra is a small hand-held harp called a lyre that was popular in ancient Greece.

STAR SEARCH

Vega (VAY-guh or VEE-guh) means "falling" in Arabic, and the Arabs thought of the star as a bird falling from the sky. This nearby star is only 27 light-years away, which is part of the reason it appears so bright. In reality it is 50 times as bright as our sun. Notice the contrast of Vega's bluish color with the yellowish color of Arcturus to the west. Vega is the fifth brightest star in the sky. It will be the North Star in about 12,500 years.

SUMMER TRIANGLE

Vega is the westernmost of three bright stars that form the Summer Triangle (see Star Chart 9, page 71). Although it is not an official constellation (it is made of stars from three different constellations), the Summer Triangle is so easy to recognize that it is the first star pattern most people find in the summer sky. Once you locate the Summer Triangle, you can find your way around much of the sky.

As you would expect, the Summer Triangle is at its best in the summertime, but it is visible most of the year. It is in the east late in the evening in June and in the west early in the evening at the end of December.

The other two stars of the Summer Triangle are Deneb in Cygnus and Altair in Aquila.

GET A LITTLE CLOSER!

A SHORT DISTANCE TO THE NORTHEAST OF VEGA IS THE STAR EPSILON—THE FAMOUS DOUBLE-DOUBLE STAR. BINOCULARS WILL SHOW TWO WIDELY SEPARATED STARS WHERE YOUR

EYES SEE ONE. A TELESCOPE USED WITH HIGH POWER SHOWS THAT EACH OF THESE TWO STARS IS ITSELF ACTUALLY A PAIR OF STARS VERY CLOSE TO EACH OTHER, MAKING FOUR IN ALL.

Mensa Table Mountain (see Star Charts 16, page 74 & 17, page 75)

Mensa (MEN-suh), Latin for "table," is named after a flat-topped hill called Table Mountain that is near Cape Town, South Africa. It was named by the French astronomer Lacaille, who observed it from the mountain in the 1750s. It is near the sky's south pole and is too far to the south to be seen from the United States. You're not missing much—it is a small constellation of only very faint stars.

Microscopium the Microscope
(see Star Charts 15 & 16, page 74; & 18, page 75)

Lacaille loved to place machines in the sky when he created new constellations in the 1750s. The Microscope is one of the few of his star patterns that is far enough north to be seen from the United States. It is a group of dim stars that lies straight south of Capricornus. Like Capricornus, **Microscopium (my-kruh-SCOH-pee-um)** is in the evening sky in early autumn.

Monoceros the Unicorn (see Star Chart 12, page 72)

Made up of only faint stars, the Unicorn is often overlooked, because it is next to some of the brightest constellations in the sky. It sits to the left of Orion and between the Big Dog and the Little Dog in the winter sky.

A unicorn is an imaginary horselike animal with one straight horn coming out of its forehead. **Monoceros (mah-NOH-sir-ahss)** was invented by the Dutch map maker Petrus Plancius in 1613.

The Milky Way runs through Monoceros, and if you have a telescope, there are many interesting star clusters within its boundaries.

Musca the Fly (see Star Charts 17 & 18, page 75)

Musca (MUSS-kuh) is a small constellation that lies straight south of the Southern Cross—too far south to see from the United States. Musca was once called Apis the Bee but was renamed the Fly by Lacaille in the 1750s.

Norma the Carpenter's Square (see Star Chart 18, page 75)

This very small group of stars lies so far to the south that it cannot be seen from the northern United States, and from the southern states it is near the southern horizon, below the front part of Scorpius. **Norma (NOR-muh)** is a small ring of faint stars. The best time to see it is early on July evenings.

A carpenter's square is a tool that looks like a large letter *L* and is used to make sure that angles are correct. The constellation looks nothing like any kind of square. It was named by Lacaille in the 1750s.

Octans the Octant
(see Star Charts 16, page 74 & 18, page 75)

This small constellation, **Octans (AHK-tans),** is directly above the earth's South Pole. It cannot be seen from the Northern Hemisphere, but (like Ursa Minor) it never sets from the Southern Hemisphere. It has only very faint stars, one of which is Sigma—the closest star to the sky's south pole. Sigma is 16 times fainter than the North Star.

An octant is an antique navigational device that was used to find the positions of ships at sea. Lacaille named this constellation in the 1750s.

Ophiuchus the Serpent Bearer (see Star Chart 14, page 73)

This outline of a man occupies a large area of the summer sky north of Scorpius. **Ophiuchus (OH-fee-YOO-kuss)** is holding a snake (a serpent), which is the constellation Serpens, in his bare hands. The serpent's head is to the right of Ophiuchus, his tail is to the left, and his body seems to cross in front of Ophiuchus. One constellation cannot be in front of another, so Ophiuchus divides the snake into two parts—the head and the tail. No constellations are more closely connected than the snake handler and his serpent.

Ophiuchus is high in the south in early evening through July and August. With a bit of imagination it is not hard to see the outline of a giant man, even though he has no especially bright stars.

According to modern constellation boundaries, the sun passes through the southern edge of Ophiuchus, making it a constellation of the zodiac. Ophiuchus is not part of the traditional astrological zodiac of 12 equally spaced signs, but it is the 13th constellation of the astronomical zodiac.

Ophiuchus is a doctor. The Greeks knew him by the name of Aesculapius, and he was a superphysician who tried the ultimate medical skill: reviving the dead. This alarmed Pluto, god of the underworld, who was afraid he'd receive no new visitors. Pluto protested to the god Zeus, who banished Aesculapius to the sky. When physicians take the Hippocratic oath today, they begin by swearing to Aesculapius (Ophiuchus) to do their duty.

Orion the Hunter (see Star Charts 11 & 12, page 72)

Orion (uh-RYE-un) is the most magnificent constellation in the sky and is one of the few constellations that looks like what it is named after.

The first thing people see of Orion is his belt, which is a straight line of three bright equally spaced stars. These stars are, from right to left, Mintaka, Alnilam, and Alnitak ("girdle," "string of pearls," and "belt," respectively, in Arabic). In some countries they are associated with the three wise men who visited the baby Jesus.

His shoulders are the stars Betelgeuse (BAY-tuhl-juice) at left and Bellatrix (bell-AH-triks) at right. Orion's head is a tiny group of three stars.

A sword hangs from his belt. The sword is a string of many faint stars close together. A bright nebula, or cloud of gas, is the sword's jewel.

His knees or legs are the stars Saiph (sah-IF) and Rigel

GET A LITTLE CLOSER!

THE JEWEL IN ORION'S SWORD IS THE BRIGHTEST NEBULA IN THE SKY. THE WORD *NEBULA* IS LATIN FOR "CLOUD," AND THIS NEBULA IS AN ENORMOUS CLOUD OF HYDROGEN GAS DOZENS OF LIGHT-YEARS ACROSS AND 1,600 LIGHT-YEARS FROM EARTH. IT IS A PLACE WHERE STARS ARE CONTINUALLY

BEING BORN, AND INSIDE IT YOU CAN SEE SEVERAL BRAND-NEW STARS THAT ARE LIGHTING UP THE NEBULA. THE ORION NEBULA (M42) IS VISIBLE WITHOUT A TELESCOPE IF THE SKY IS DARK, AND IT IS ONE OF THE MOST POPULAR TARGETS FOR YOUNG ASTRONOMERS.

(RYE-jull). *Saiph* is Arabic for "sword" (even though the star is in the wrong place to actually be Orion's sword), and *Rigel* is Arabic for "foot."

Orion faces to the right (west). He holds a shield in front—a long string of faint stars that stretches up toward the red star Aldebaran in the Bull. In his other hand he holds a club—two strings of faint stars that extend toward the feet of Gemini. The club is over his head as if about to strike. The shield and club are not easy to see unless the sky is very dark.

Orion is in the evening sky from December through March, although you can see him late at night as early as August. When you see Orion in the southeast in the evening, winter is about to begin.

Orion was a giant and a hunter who had many adventures. In one Greek myth he boasted he could kill any animal alive. This offended the gods, who sent a scorpion to kill him. Orion and the scorpion (the constellation Scorpius) were then placed in the sky—but on opposite sides. Orion is in the winter sky and Scorpius is in the summer, and one rises while the other sets.

GIANTS IN THE SKY?

Orion has two of the brightest stars in the sky. They are giants—Betelgeuse (which comes from "hand of the giant" in Arabic) is a red supergiant, and Rigel a blue supergiant. The color contrast between them is striking. Although called a red giant, Betelgeuse is actually orange in color.

Betelgeuse is an enormous star. If we replaced our sun with it, the orbits of the planets Mercury, Venus, earth, and Mars would fit inside it! Betelgeuse is unstable and slowly changes its size and brightness. It is 10,000 times as bright as our sun and about 520 light-years away.

The gruesome but funny movie and cartoon character whose name is pronounced "beetle juice" was named after the star.

Rigel is the seventh brightest star in the sky. It is about 50,000 times as bright as our sun and about the same size as Betelgeuse. It is 900 light-years away.

Pavo the Peacock (see Star Charts 16, page 74 & 18, page 75)

Pavo (PAH-voh) the Peacock first appeared on Bayer's atlas in 1603. It lies so far to the south that from the southern United States you can see only its northernmost star. Its other stars are quite faint. It is far south of Sagittarius and Capricornus.

Pegasus
the Flying or Winged Horse
(see Star Chart 4, page 68)

Pegasus (PEH-guh-suss) is a trio of three equally bright stars and a sprinkling of much fainter stars nearby. Most people see Pegasus as a large square of four stars called the Great Square of Pegasus, a pattern of bright stars in the autumn sky. However, the Great Square is not the same as Pegasus, since its northeast star is actually in the constellation Andromeda.

   You can visualize the stars of Pegasus as the front part of a horse. He is flying upside down.

   According to Greek mythology, Pegasus was created by Poseidon, the god of the oceans. He made this strange winged horse out of blood from Medusa's head that had dripped into the sea. Pegasus was later flown by Perseus. (See Andromeda for the full story.)

IS THE GREAT SQUARE REALLY SQUARE?

Not exactly. Its sides vary between 13 degrees and 16 degrees long—but that is close to a square, at least as far as stars are concerned. Without binoculars, the square looks empty of stars.

53

Perseus the Hero
(see Star Charts 1, page 67 & 5, page 69)

Perseus (PURR-see-us) lies midway between Cassiopeia and Taurus in the winter sky. When he is at his highest, he is overhead or even north of overhead for viewers in the United States.

It is easiest to see Perseus as a long curving string of stars. The brightest star, Alpha, is in a straight line with the three stars of Andromeda. The string begins south of the easternmost part of the W that forms Cassiopeia.

The faintest part of the Milky Way passes through Perseus, and many dim stars and nice clusters of stars are within its boundaries.

It was Perseus who rescued Andromeda from Cetus and received the thanks of Cassiopeia and Cepheus. (See Andromeda for the full story.)

METEORS FROM PERSEUS

Each summer for a few days around August 12 the earth moves through a swarm of dust shed by a comet long ago. That dust falls through our atmosphere as a shower of meteors. The meteors appear all over the sky, but because they come from the direction of Perseus, they are called Perseid meteors. Look from a dark location (maybe you'll be on vacation then) and you might see a few dozen meteors in one night!

Phoenix the Phoenix or Firebird (see Star Chart 16, page 74)

This constellation was created by Bayer to "use up" faint stars not included in other constellations. It is far south of the constellation Cetus and visible from the southernmost United States.

Phoenix (FEE-niks) is named after a mythical bird, a

symbol of rebirth. In Egyptian mythology a phoenix is a type of bird that lives for 500 years and then sets itself on fire and dies. It is reborn from its ashes.

Pictor the Painter's Easel
(see Star Charts 16, page 74 & 17, page 75)

Lacaille created this small constellation in the 1750s while he was in South Africa. **Pictor (PIK-tor)** lies a short distance to the right of the very bright star Canopus. It is too far south to see from any place north of Hawaii or Miami.

Pisces the Fishes (see Star Chart 4, page 68)

Pisces (PIE-seez) is a large zodiacal constellation of mostly faint stars in the autumn and winter sky. It is two fish swimming in opposite directions with their tails tied together.

While there are ancient myths about the fish and their adventures, little information exists that tells us why these stars were originally named fish. In one Greek myth the fishes' tails were tied together so they would not be separated. We still see them this way today.

Piscis Austrinus the Southern Fish
(see Star Charts 10, page 71; & 15 & 16, page 74)

This constellation is unusual in that it has one bright star, plus some very dim stars. It is practically a one-star constellation.

Piscis Austrinus (PIE-sis AWS-truh-nuss) is to the lower left of Capricornus and can be seen in fall.

Fomalhaut (FOH-muhl-hote)—the Southern Fish's bright star and 18th brightest star in the sky—guides the way to the nearby faint constellations Grus, Cetus, and Aquarius.

Puppis the Stern (see Star Chart 17, page 75)

The astronomer Lacaille divided the star group named for Greek hero Jason's ancient and huge ship the *Argo*, once the largest constellation, into three: Vela, Carina, and **Puppis (PUH-piss)**. Puppis is the ship's Stern.

Puppis is below and to the lower right of Canis Major and between the two brightest stars in the sky, Sirius and Canopus. It has quite a few medium-bright stars, but it is hard to see them as part of a ship. You can view it in the winter.

Pyxis the nautical Compass
(see Star Charts 12, page 72 & 17, page 75)

When Lacaille created three constellations out of the ship *Argo*, he added **Pyxis (PIK-siss)**, the ship's Compass, even though no ancient Greek sailing ship ever had a compass. Lacaille loved mechanical inventions, however, so now the old ship is guided by a modern instrument.

Pyxis has no bright stars. It is a short string of faint stars to the left of Puppis and above the sail, approximately where a ship's compass should be. Like Puppis, it is in the winter sky.

Reticulum the Reticule
(see Star Charts 16, page 74 & 17, page 75)

Reticulum (re-TIK-yoo-lum) is a small group of dim stars near the sky's south pole—too far south to see from the United States.

Lacaille named if after a reticule, the kind of telescope eyepiece he used to measure star positions during his stay in South Africa in the 1750s.

Sagitta the Arrow (see Star Chart 9, page 71)

The word *sagitta* (sa-JEET-uh) is Latin for "arrow," and this small group of stars certainly does look like an arrow in the sky. It is the third smallest constellation, but it is surprisingly easy to see. Look for it north of Altair, the southernmost star of the Summer Triangle. It is one fourth of the way from Altair toward Deneb in Cygnus. It is in the evening sky in summer and early fall.

You can imagine that this is an arrow fired by the constellation Sagittarius, to the south, toward the two birds Aquila the Eagle and Cygnus the Swan. It seems he missed both!

Sagittarius the Archer

(see Star Charts 14, page 73; 15, page 74; & 18, page 75)

You can view Sagittarius as a teapot:

1. Four stars at the left end are the handle.

2. The top is a triangle of three stars above.

3. The spout is outlined by three stars to the right.

4. A short line of faint stars above the handle is the teaspoon. (And Corona Australis below is the lemon!)

The Archer is a prominent and ancient constellation that has many bright stars. You can see **Sagittarius (sa-juh-TAIR-ee-us)** in summer and early fall evenings, when it is low in the south.

A constellation of the zodiac, Sagittarius is a centaur. However, most people see Sagittarius as a teapot: When Sagittarius is in

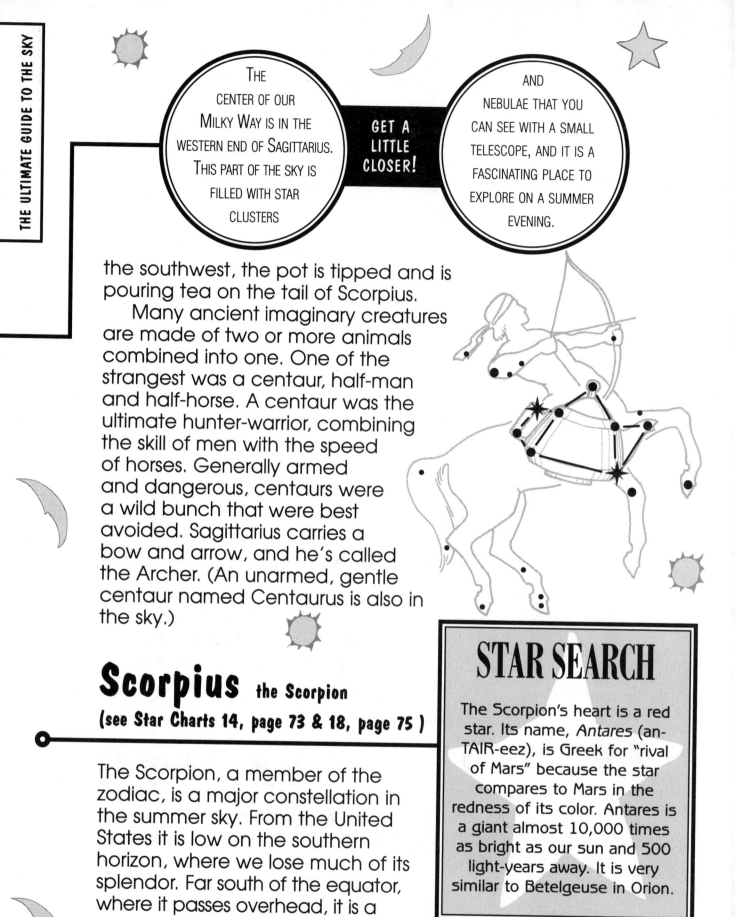

THE CENTER OF OUR MILKY WAY IS IN THE WESTERN END OF SAGITTARIUS. THIS PART OF THE SKY IS FILLED WITH STAR CLUSTERS

GET A LITTLE CLOSER!

AND NEBULAE THAT YOU CAN SEE WITH A SMALL TELESCOPE, AND IT IS A FASCINATING PLACE TO EXPLORE ON A SUMMER EVENING.

the southwest, the pot is tipped and is pouring tea on the tail of Scorpius.

Many ancient imaginary creatures are made of two or more animals combined into one. One of the strangest was a centaur, half-man and half-horse. A centaur was the ultimate hunter-warrior, combining the skill of men with the speed of horses. Generally armed and dangerous, centaurs were a wild bunch that were best avoided. Sagittarius carries a bow and arrow, and he's called the Archer. (An unarmed, gentle centaur named Centaurus is also in the sky.)

Scorpius the Scorpion
(see Star Charts 14, page 73 & 18, page 75)

The Scorpion, a member of the zodiac, is a major constellation in the summer sky. From the United States it is low on the southern horizon, where we lose much of its splendor. Far south of the equator, where it passes overhead, it is a

STAR SEARCH

The Scorpion's heart is a red star. Its name, *Antares* (an-TAIR-eez), is Greek for "rival of Mars" because the star compares to Mars in the redness of its color. Antares is a giant almost 10,000 times as bright as our sun and 500 light-years away. It is very similar to Betelgeuse in Orion.

magnificent group of bright stars.

Scorpius (SKOR-pee-us) truly looks like a scorpion, and people have been calling it the Scorpion since prehistoric times—at least 6,000 years.

Scorpius now has only three stars for stubby claws, but long ago the claws included the stars of Libra, to the right.

In Greek mythology Scorpius was the enemy of Orion. Orion died from the scorpion's bite. Both he and the scorpion were placed in the sky, but on opposite sides, so one sets while the other rises.

The Milky Way runs through Scorpius. Like Sagittarius, it is filled with star clusters that are visible in binoculars or a small telescope. Two star clusters, M6 and M7, are bright enough to see without binoculars. They lie between the Scorpion's stinger and the western end of Sagittarius.

Sculptor the Sculptor's Workshop
(see Star Charts 10, page 71 & 16, page 74)

This faint constellation, **Sculptor (SKULP-tor),** lies south of Aquarius and Cetus in the autumn sky. Look for it as a shapeless group of dim stars to the left of the bright star Fomalhaut, in the Southern Fish. The Sculptor's Workshop was created by Lacaille in the 1750s.

Scutum the Shield (see Star Charts 14, page 73 & 15, page 74)

The Shield is a group of faint stars with no particular shape. It lies between Aquila, Sagittarius, and Ophiuchus in the summer sky.

Scutum (SKYOO-tum) was named by Hevelius in honor of John Sobieski, the king of Poland, who defeated the Turks

in a major battle only seven years earlier. Originally called Scutum Sobiescianum, the name has since been shortened.

Within Scutum is the star cluster M11, best viewed through a telescope. It contains hundreds of stars and is about 5,000 light-years from earth.

Serpens the Serpent or Snake (see Star Chart 14, page 73)

Serpens (SIR-pens) is unusual in that it is divided into two separate pieces in the sky with a constellation between them. Ophiuchus, the handler, is holding a giant snake in outstretched hands. The snake's head is to the right of Ophiuchus and its tail is to the left, and the two parts are called Serpens Caput and Serpens Cauda from the Latin words for head and tail, respectively. You are supposed to imagine that the middle part of the snake "crosses" Ophiuchus's body. Since one constellation cannot be in front of another, poor Serpens is divided in two.

When you spot Serpens, you will see that it does look like a snake. Serpens's head is a circle of faint stars near the constellation Corona Borealis. Its body extends to the south, and then it bends eastward. It "crosses" Ophiuchus in a straight line, and then "snakes" up and to the left, ending in a faint star.

Serpens is visible in the southern sky during the early evening in July and August.

Sextans the Sextant
(see Star Charts 6, page 69; 12, page 72; & 13, page 73)

This little constellation, **Sextans (SEKS-tanz),** contains only faint stars and is barely visible. It is straight south of Leo and can be seen in the United States in the springtime.

Hevelius named it in 1690 after the sextant, an instrument used to measure the positions of stars.

Taurus the Bull (see Star Chart 5, page 69)

Taurus (TORE-us) is one of the major constellations of the winter sky. It contains three bright stars and—even more importantly —two very bright star clusters. The Bull is above and to the right of Orion the Hunter, who is fighting the Bull and driving it westward across the sky.

Taurus looks like the front end of a giant bull.

STAR CLUSTERS IN THE BULL

Two prominent clusters, Hyades (HI-uh-deez) and Pleiades (PLEE-uh-deez), are so clear they can be seen by the naked eye.

The Bull's face is the Hyades. The cluster looks even more impressive through binoculars, but a telescope does not improve the view. Many of its stars are red and yellow, and this is in contrast with the younger Pleiades, which has blue and white stars. The Hyades lies 150 light-years from earth.

Aldebaran lies between the earth and the stars of the Hyades and is not part of the cluster.

The Pleiades rises an hour before the rest of Taurus. To the early Greeks in the seventh century B.C. the Pleiades was considered a separate constellation, but now it is part of the bull. Although the Pleiades are also called Seven Sisters, there are six bright and many more faint stars. You might see as many as a dozen if your eyesight is exceptionally good, but binoculars will show many more. In Greek mythology the Seven Sisters were targets of Orion's affection, and he pursues them endlessly across the sky.

The Pleiades is 360 light-years from earth and 7 light-years across. It looks like a very little dipper.

Taurus, a zodiacal constellation, is usually shown with its hindquarters missing. It has been known as the Bull since prehistoric times and was worshipped in ancient Egypt as the god Apis. It also appears in Greek mythology, where the god Zeus disguises himself as the Bull when he visits his mortal lady friends on earth.

Here's how to see Taurus:

1. The bright red star Aldebaran is one fiery eye.

2. The Bull's face is a V-shaped group of bright stars near Aldebaran. This group is called the Hyades. Its other eye is among these stars.

3. The Bull's horns extend up and to the left and end in two bright stars that are directly above Orion.

4. Its back is a little cluster of stars called the Pleiades, or Seven Sisters.

Telescopium
the Telescope (see Star Charts 16, page 74 & 18, page 75)

The Telescope appears as a small triangle of stars to the lower right of the tail of Scorpius. **Telescopium (tell-uh-SKOH-pee-um)** is too far to the south to be seen well from the United States. It was invented by Lacaille to honor telescopes, and it has no mythology associated with it.

Triangulum the Triangle
(see Star Charts 4, page 68 & 5, page 69)

The Triangle is below Andromeda and above Aries, and it is visible in the autumn. Although made of rather faint stars, it is easy to see because of its simple triangular shape.

Triangulum (try-AN-gyoo-lum) was invented by the ancient Greeks, who loved geometry.

The bright, nearby spiral galaxy M33 is in the northern part of Triangulum. It can be seen with binoculars on a dark night.

Triangulum Australe
the Southern Triangle (see Star Chart 18, page 75)

The Southern Triangle is a group of three bright stars east of Alpha Centauri and near the sky's south pole. Although **Triangulum Australe (try-AN-gyoo-lum aws-TRAY-lee)** is easy to see from the Southern Hemisphere, it cannot be seen from the United States.

Tucana   the Toucan (see Star Chart 16, page 74)

A toucan, for which this constellation is named, is a large colorful bird with a big bill that lives in the tropics of South America. **Tucana (too-CAN-uh)** is a group of stars that "lives" near the sky's south pole, too far south to be seen from the United States. In 1603 it was introduced by Bayer, who apparently was fascinated by strange new objects from the New World.

Ursa Major   the Great Bear
(see Star Charts 2, page 67 & 3, page 68)

The Great Bear, **Ursa Major (ER-suh MAY-jer)**, is the third largest constellation. It contains the seven stars known as the Big Dipper plus many fainter stars. It is seen best in the spring, but much of it is always visible.

If these stars don't look much like a bear, why is it called a bear? Perhaps people long ago noticed that these stars *act* like a bear. They rise in the spring, when bears come out of hibernation, and they set in the fall, when bears disappear for the winter. During the winter the celestial bear is low in the north and out of sight.

Perhaps the most curious aspect of the Great Bear is why it was called a bear by people in such widely separated places as Europe, Siberia, and North America. There are two possibilities. Either these people independently thought up the idea that these stars should be a bear, or the idea of the Great Bear was carried far and wide as people migrated more than 10,000 years ago. If this second reason is correct, as many people believe, the idea of calling these stars a bear dates back to the Ice Age and is one of the oldest human creations that still exists.

The two end stars in the Dipper's bowl are called the Pointer Stars because they point to the North Star. Draw a line through them and continue one dipper's length northward to reach the North Star.

To see Ursa Major as a bear:

1. Find the Big Dipper. The handle of the Dipper is the Bear's long tail and the bowl is the hind part of its body.

2. The Bear's neck and head is a group of faint stars almost one dipper's length to the west.

3. Its feet are more faint stars to the south and west. If you have a better-than-average imagination, you might see a bear.

IS THE BIG DIPPER A CONSTELLATION?

No, but the seven brightest stars of the Great Bear constellation make up this most familiar group of stars.

These seven stars are called a dipper only in the United States and Canada. In England they are a plow, in Germany they are Charles's Wagon (Wain), and in France they are a casserole pot. In ancient Egypt they were the leg of a bull.

Strangely no one knows how these stars came to be called a dipper. Perhaps the idea was brought from Africa by slaves, who used to drink from dippers made from hollowed gourds. Before the Civil War, slaves called the Big Dipper the Drinking Gourd.

Ursa Minor

the Small Bear
(see Star Charts 2, page 67 & 3, page 68)

The Small Bear looks even less like a bear than the Great Bear. What people see is the Little Dipper— a pattern of seven stars that does look like a scoop, or dipper. The brightest of its stars is Polaris (poh-LAIR-us), the North Star, and the only two other bright stars are at the end of the bowl. The four stars between are quite faint, and it takes a dark sky to see the entire Little Dipper. The Little Dipper plus a few very faint stars nearby make up **Ursa Minor (ER-suh MY-ner).** From the United States and Canada the Small Bear remains above the northern horizon and it never sets. The Dipper's bowl is highest in early summer.

STAR SEARCH

Polaris is a star that is famous because of *where* it is rather than *what* it is. There is nothing special about this star, but it happens to lie directly above the North Pole of the earth. The earth's axis points to it. As the earth turns and the sky rotates overhead, the North Star stays in one place, and the sky turns around it. To find north, simply face the North Star. The North Star is represented by the paper clip or small piece of wire on your Rotating Star Finder.

Vela the Sail (see Star Chart 17, page 75)

Vela (VEE-luh) has many bright stars, but it is so far to the south that only its northern part can be seen from the United States. It lies to the lower left of Canis Major and left of the bright star Canopus.

Vela is the sail of the huge ship *Argo* that Lacaille divided into three smaller constellations in the 1750s.

Virgo the Virgin or Young Maiden
(see Star Charts 13 & 14, page 73)

Virgo (VER-go) is the second largest constellation. This member of the zodiac is in the evening sky in late spring and early summer.

Virgo is a young maiden who is associated with agriculture and especially with planting and with ploughing the first furrow of spring, when a barren field is seeded and becomes fertile.

Volans the Flying Fish (see Star Chart 17, page 75)

The Flying Fish is between Carina (the Keel) and the sky's south pole—too far to the south to be seen from the United States. It has no bright stars. **Volans (VOH-lanz)** was created by Bayer in 1603.

Vulpecula the Fox (see Star Chart 9, page 71)

The Fox lies between Cygnus and Sagitta in the summer sky. It was created by Hevelius in 1690 and has only very faint stars. **Vulpecula (vuhl-PEK-yoo-luh)** has one claim to fame—the Dumbbell Nebula situated within its borders. The Dumbbell, also known as M27, is a cloud of gas shed by a dying star long ago, and it is easily visible through a small telescope.

CHAPTER 4

THE STAR CHARTS

The following charts are what you will need to locate specific constellations on your Rotating Star Finder. Turn to pages 13 through 15 for an explanation of how to use the charts. (The gray background on some of the charts marks the Milky Way galaxy.)

Star Chart 1

Star Chart 2

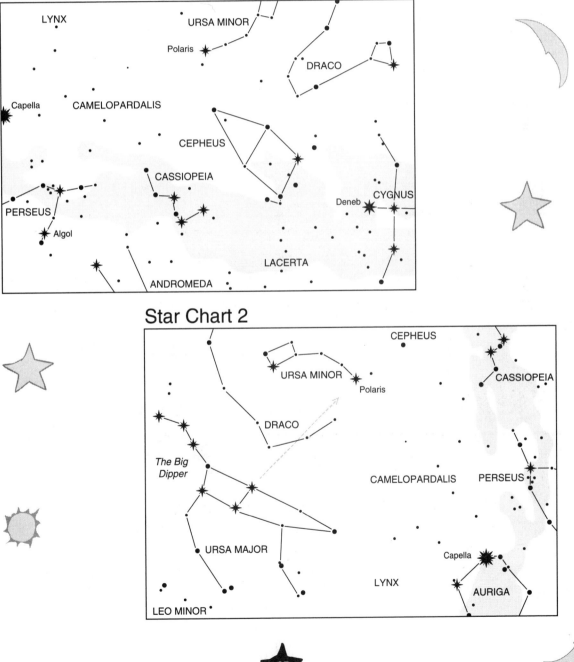

Star Chart 3

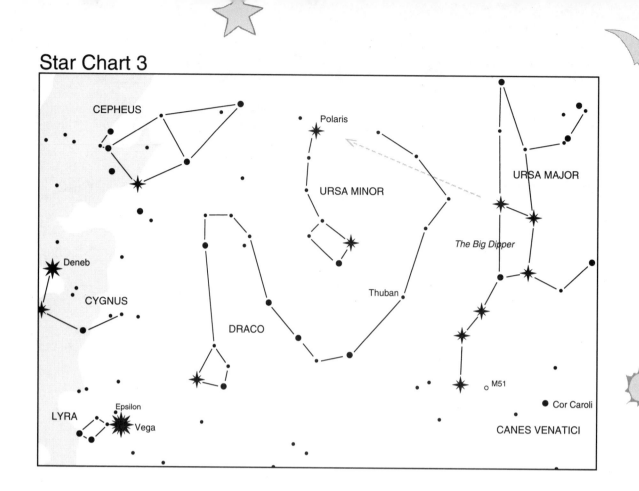

CEPHEUS

Polaris

URSA MINOR

URSA MAJOR

The Big Dipper

Deneb

CYGNUS

Thuban

DRACO

M51

Cor Caroli

LYRA

Epsilon

Vega

CANES VENATICI

Star Chart 4

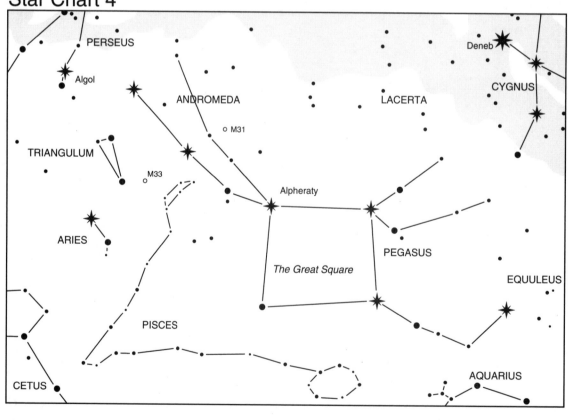

PERSEUS

Algol

ANDROMEDA

LACERTA

Deneb

CYGNUS

M31

TRIANGULUM

M33

Alpheraty

ARIES

PEGASUS

The Great Square

EQUULEUS

PISCES

AQUARIUS

CETUS

Star Chart 5

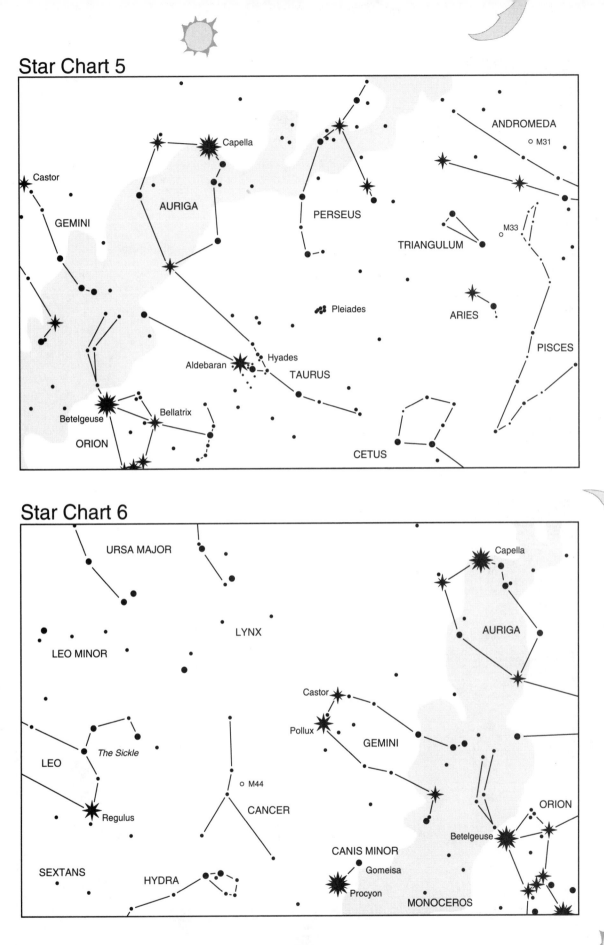

Star Chart 6

Star Chart 7

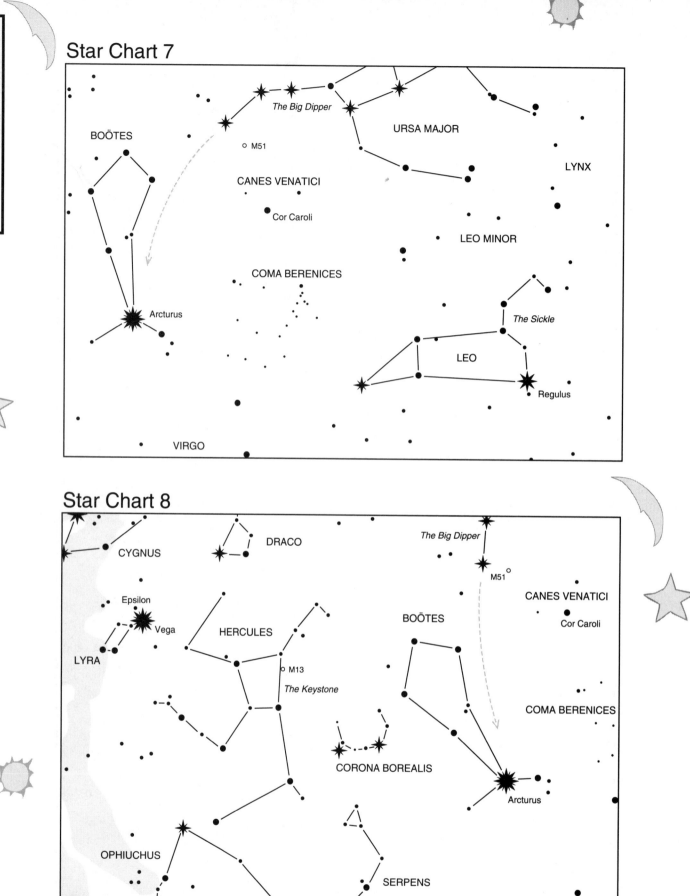

BOÖTES

The Big Dipper

URSA MAJOR

LYNX

○ M51

CANES VENATICI

Cor Caroli

LEO MINOR

COMA BERENICES

The Sickle

Arcturus

LEO

Regulus

VIRGO

Star Chart 8

CYGNUS

DRACO

The Big Dipper

M51 ○

CANES VENATICI

Epsilon

Vega

HERCULES

BOÖTES

Cor Caroli

LYRA

○ M13

The Keystone

COMA BERENICES

CORONA BOREALIS

Arcturus

OPHIUCHUS

SERPENS

70

Star Chart 9

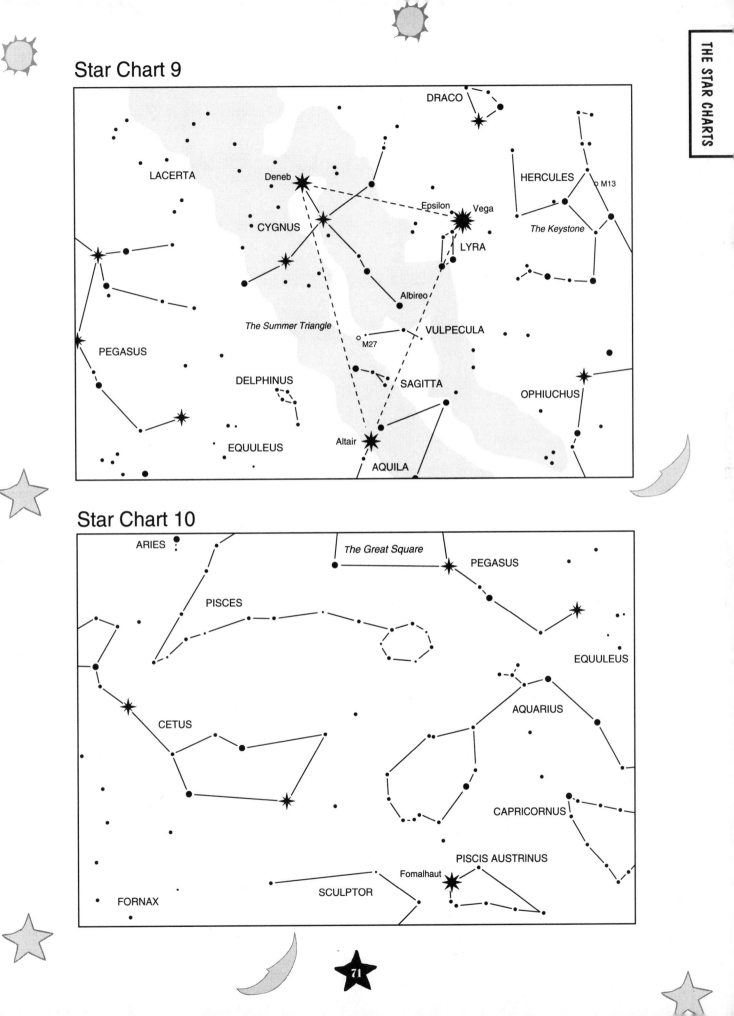

DRACO

LACERTA

Deneb

Epsilon

Vega

CYGNUS

LYRA

HERCULES

M13

The Keystone

Albireo

VULPECULA

The Summer Triangle

M27

PEGASUS

DELPHINUS

SAGITTA

OPHIUCHUS

Altair

EQUULEUS

AQUILA

Star Chart 10

ARIES

The Great Square

PEGASUS

PISCES

EQUULEUS

AQUARIUS

CETUS

CAPRICORNUS

PISCIS AUSTRINUS

Fomalhaut

SCULPTOR

FORNAX

Star Chart 11

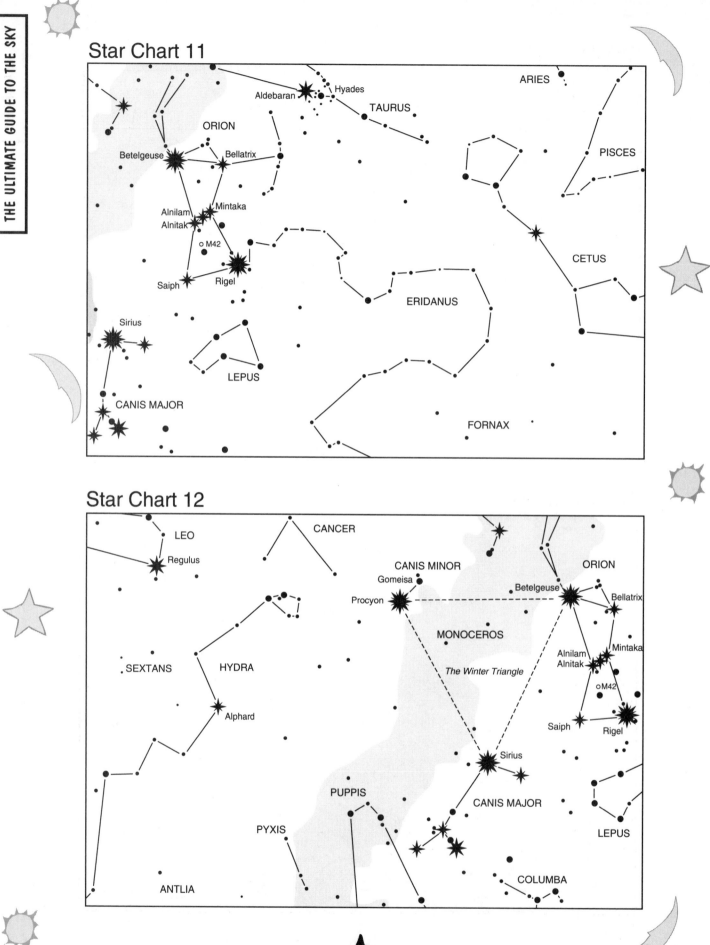

Star Chart 12

Star Chart 13

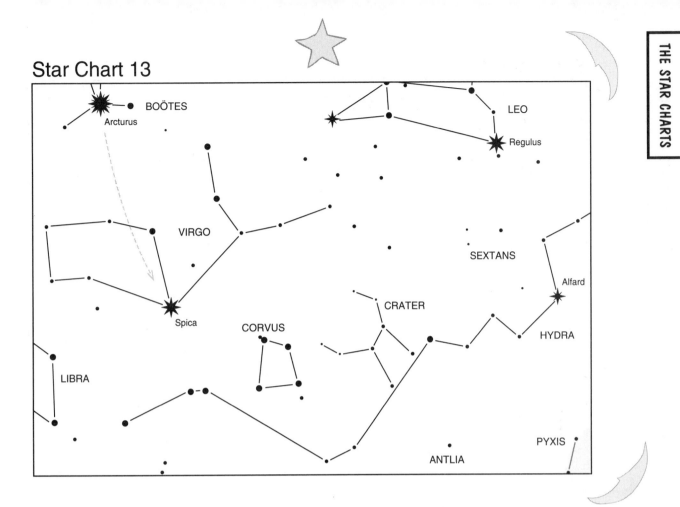

BOÖTES
Arcturus
LEO
Regulus
VIRGO
SEXTANS
Alfard
CRATER
CORVUS
Spica
HYDRA
LIBRA
PYXIS
ANTLIA

Star Chart 14

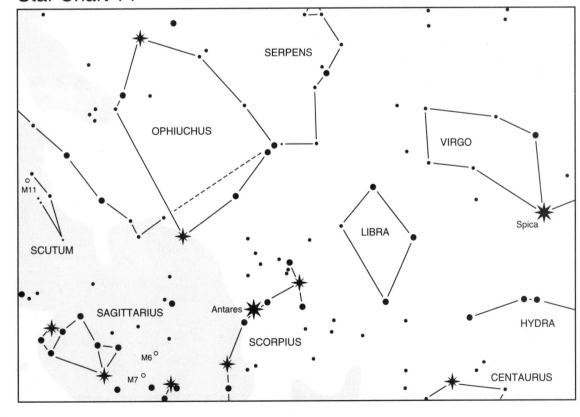

SERPENS
OPHIUCHUS
VIRGO
Spica
M11
LIBRA
SCUTUM
HYDRA
SAGITTARIUS
Antares
M6
SCORPIUS
CENTAURUS
M7

Star Chart 15

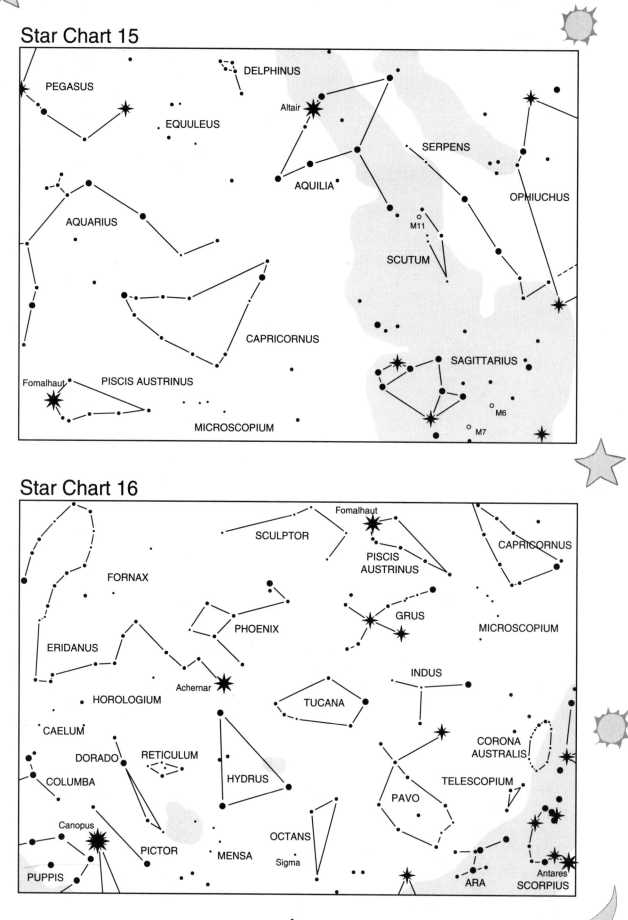

PEGASUS

DELPHINUS

EQUULEUS

Altair

SERPENS

AQUILIA

OPHIUCHUS

AQUARIUS

M11

SCUTUM

CAPRICORNUS

SAGITTARIUS

Fomalhaut

PISCIS AUSTRINUS

M6

MICROSCOPIUM

M7

Star Chart 16

SCULPTOR

Fomalhaut

CAPRICORNUS

PISCIS
AUSTRINUS

FORNAX

PHOENIX

GRUS

MICROSCOPIUM

ERIDANUS

Achernar

INDUS

HOROLOGIUM

TUCANA

CAELUM

CORONA
AUSTRALIS

DORADO

RETICULUM

HYDRUS

TELESCOPIUM

COLUMBA

PAVO

Canopus

OCTANS

PICTOR

MENSA

Sigma

PUPPIS

ARA

Antares

SCORPIUS

Star Chart 17

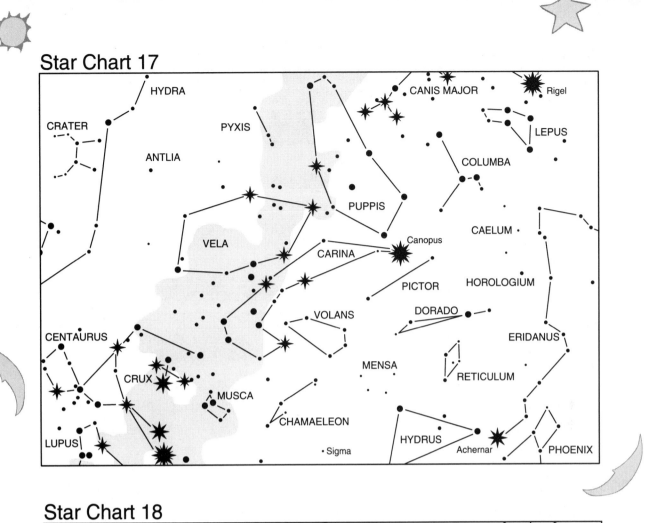

HYDRA

CRATER

PYXIS

ANTLIA

CANIS MAJOR

Rigel

LEPUS

COLUMBA

PUPPIS

VELA

CARINA

CAELUM

Canopus

PICTOR

HOROLOGIUM

VOLANS

DORADO

ERIDANUS

CENTAURUS

MENSA

RETICULUM

CRUX

MUSCA

CHAMAELEON

HYDRUS

Achernar

PHOENIX

LUPUS

Sigma

Star Chart 18

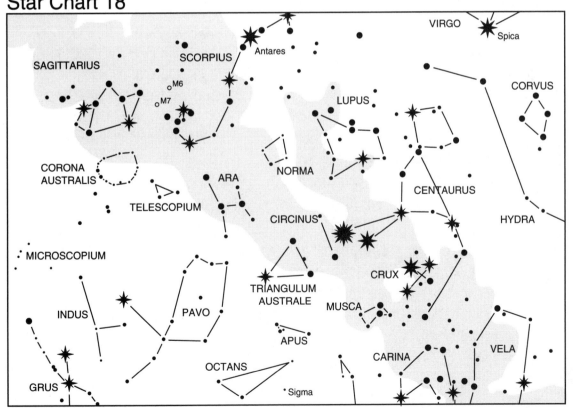

SAGITTARIUS

SCORPIUS

Antares

VIRGO

Spica

M6

M7

CORVUS

LUPUS

CORONA
AUSTRALIS

ARA

NORMA

CENTAURUS

TELESCOPIUM

CIRCINUS

HYDRA

MICROSCOPIUM

CRUX

INDUS

PAVO

TRIANGULUM
AUSTRALE

MUSCA

APUS

GRUS

OCTANS

CARINA

VELA

Sigma

CHAPTER 5

WHAT TO DO NEXT?

You've learned many of the constellations. You've studied the brightest stars, and even watched the planets move slowly throughout the year. But you're ready for more. What now?

Begin at your local planetarium. If there is not a planetarium in your town, there is one in a nearby city. A planetarium creates an indoor night sky where you can observe the constellations, as well as learn about the latest discoveries in astronomy. It might also have an astronomy museum and bookstore. Planetariums exist to help people learn about the stars, and the staff will be happy to answer your questions.

Join an astronomy club. There is no better way to become an expert at something than by hanging out with people who are knowledgeable and enthusiastic. Astronomy clubs often conduct "star parties," where the members gather to look at the sky through a variety of telescopes. Your local planetarium or museum will know about astronomy clubs in your area.

Subscribe to an astronomy magazine. One excellent magazine for young people is *Odyssey*, published monthly by Cobblestone Publishing, 7 School St., Peterborough, NH 03458.

Check out astronomy computer programs. If you have a personal computer, explore the sky without ever leaving your house! Astronomy computer programs show the positions of the stars and planets at any time, the constellations in great detail, and they simulate eclipses and the motions of the planets.

Explore the World Wide Web. A universe of astronomy information is available for free on the Internet's World Wide Web—even on cloudy nights, when you cannot see the stars! You'll find information and software.

Good places to start (with links to other sites) are:

Sky and Telescope magazine at:

http://www.skypub.com

Astronomy magazine at:

http://www.kalmbach.com/astro/astronomy.html

"Stars and Constellations" at:

http://www.astro.wisc.edu/~dolan/constellations

Links to selected astronomy sites are at the Griffith Observatory's web site at:

http://www.GriffithObs.org.

GLOSSARY

astronomer A person who studies and knows about the sky and the stars, planets, and other things it contains.

atlas A set of charts or maps.

cartographer One who makes maps.

circumpolar The area of the sky centered on the North Star is so far to the north that it never sets and is visible all night.

constellation An area of the sky or a pattern of stars in a certain area. There are 88 official constellations.

ecliptic The path in the sky the sun seems to follow as it moves around the sky once a year. The ecliptic is the blue circle on your Rotating Star Finder.

galaxy A huge system of billions of stars lying millions of light-years away. The earth is in the Milky Way galaxy.

giant star A very big star that is many times the size of our sun.

Johann Bayer A lawyer and amateur astronomer (1572–1625) who lived in Germany. His important star atlas of 1603 included letters to identify bright stars and new constellations of the southern sky.

Johannes Hevelius A beer-maker and astronomer (1611–1687) who lived in Danzig, Poland. He created several new constellations that appeared in his star atlas of 1690.

light-year The distance (not time) that light travels in one year. At the speed of 186,300 miles per second, light travels almost 6 trillion miles (5,900,000,000,000 miles) in one year.

meteor The flash of light you see when a small particle from space burns up by friction as it falls through earth's atmosphere; also called a shooting star or falling star.

Milky Way galaxy The name of the galaxy the earth is in, which is a system of hundreds of billions of stars; also, the stream of light across the sky caused by the appearance of our galaxy seen edge-on.

nebula A cloud of gas and dust that is far beyond our solar system (from the Latin word for *cloud,* as in "nebulous").

Nicolas Louis de Lacaille A French astronomer (1713–1762) who observed the southern sky from the Cape of Good Hope, South Africa, in 1751–52 and who published a chart that included new constellations he devised in 1754. He named his new constellations after instruments used in art and science.

planetarium A theater that recreates the appearance of the night sky and presents shows about discoveries in astronomy.

solar system The sun and everything that revolves around it, including the planets Mercury, Venus, earth, Mars, Jupiter, Saturn, Uranus, Neptune, and Pluto.

star atlas A set of maps that shows all the major stars and constellations in the sky.

star cluster A group of dozens to thousands of stars that were born together and that are relatively near to each other in space.

telescope An instrument with lenses or mirrors that makes distant objects look brighter and bigger.

variable star A star whose brightness changes—or varies—on a somewhat regular basis.

zodiac The band in the sky that the sun, moon, and planets travel through. Traditionally the zodiac contains 12 constellations, but the sun actually passes through 13 (and the planets pass through even more). The astronomical constellations of the zodiac are: Aries, Taurus, Gemini, Cancer, Leo, Virgo, Libra, Scorpius, Ophiuchus, Sagittarius, Capricornus, Aquarius, and Pisces.

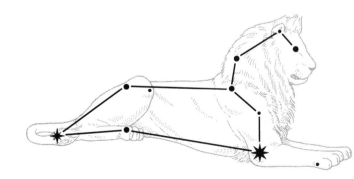

INDEX

Air Pump, 19
Altar, 21–22
American Indian, 43
Andromeda, 18–19
Antlia, 19
Apus, 20
Aquarius, 20
Aquila, 20–21
Ara, 21–22
Archer, 57–58
Argo, 28
Aries, 22
Arrow, 57
astronomy activities, 76–77
Auriga, 22–23

Bear
   Great, 63–64
   Small, 65
Berenice's Hair, 32–33
Big Dipper, 64
Bird of Paradise, 20
Bobcat, 46
Boötes, 23–24
Bull, 61–62

Caelum, 24
Camelopardalis, 24
Cancer, 24–25
Canes Venatici, 25–26
Canis Major, 26–27
Canis Minor, 27
Capricornus, 28
Carina, 28
Carpenter's Square, 49
Cassiopeia, 19, 29
Centaurus, 30
Cepheus, 30–31
Cetus, 31
Chained Maiden, 18–19
Chamaeleon, 31
Charioteer, 22–23
charts, star, 67–75
Chisel, 24
Circinus, 31

Clock, 42
Colt, 38
Columbia, 32
Coma Berenices, 32–33
Compasses, 31, 56
constellations, 18–66
   and Big Dipper, 64
   defined, 6
   movement of, 8–10
   observing, 16–17
   who invented, 10–12
Corona Australis, 33
Corona Borealis, 33–34
Corvus, 34
Crab, 24–25
Crane, 40
Crater, 34–35
Crow, 34
Crux, 35
Cygnus, 35–36

Delphinus, 36–37
Dogs
   hunting, 25–26
   large, 26–27
   small, 27
Dolphin, 36–37
Dorado, 37
Dove, 32
Draco, 37–38
Dragon, 37–38

Eagle, 20–21
Equuleus, 38
Eridanus, 38–39

Firebird, 54–55
Fly, 49
Fornax, 39
Fox, 66
Furnace, 39

Gemini, 39–40
Giraffe, 24
Greek alphabet, 10
Grus, 40

Hare, 45
Harp, 46–47
Hercules, 41
Herdsman, 23–24
Horologium, 42
Hunter, 51–52
Hydra, 42
Hydrus, 43

Indus, 43

Jason, 28

Keel, 28
King, 30–31

Lacerta, 43
Leo, 44
Leo Minor, 45
Lepus, 45
Libra, 45–46
Lion, 44
Lion, Small, 45
Lizard, 43
Lupus, 46
Lynx, 46
Lyra, 46–47

Mensa, 48
meteors from Perseus, 54
Microscope, 48
Microscopium, 48
Monoceros, 48
Musca, 49

Norma, 49
Northern Cross, 35–36
Northern Crown, 33–34

Octans, 49
Octant, 49
Ophiuchus, 50
Orion, 51–52

Painter's Easel, 55
Pavo, 53
Peacock, 53

Pegasus, 53
Perseus, 54
Phoenix, 54–55
Pictor, 55
Pisces, 55
Piscis Austrinus, 55–56
Princess, Perils of the, 19
Puppis, 56
Pyxis, 56

Queen, 29

Rabbit, 45
Ram, 22
Reticle, 56–57
Reticulum, 56–57
River, 38–39
Rotating Star Finder, 13–17

Sagitta, 57
Sagittarius, 57–58
Sail, 65
Scales, balance, 45–46
Scorpion, 58–59
Scorpius, 58–59
Sculptor, 59
Scutum, 59–60
Sea-goat, 28
Serpens, 60
Serpent, 60
Serpent Bearer, 50
Sextans, 60
Sextant, 60
Shield, 59–60
sky, giants in the, 52–54
Southern Cross, 35
Southern Crown, 33
Southern Fish, 55–56
Southern Triangle, 63
stars
   charts, 67–75
   defined, 7–8
   searches, 22–23, 25–27, 36, 47, 58, 65

studying, 5
Stern, 56
Strong Man, 41
Swan, 35–36
Swordfish, 37

Table Mountain, 48
Taurus, 61–62
Telescopium, 62
Toucan, 63
Triangulum, 62
Triangulum Australe, 63
Tucana, 63
Twins, 39–40

Ultimate Guide to the Sky, The, using, 13–17
Unicorn, 48
Ursa Major, 63–64
Ursa Minor, 65

Vela, 65
Virgo, 66
Volans, 66
Vulpecula, 66

Water Carrier, 20
Water Snake
   female, 42
   male, 43
Whale, 31
Winged Horse, 53
Wolf, 46

Young Maiden, 66

zodiac, 21, 47

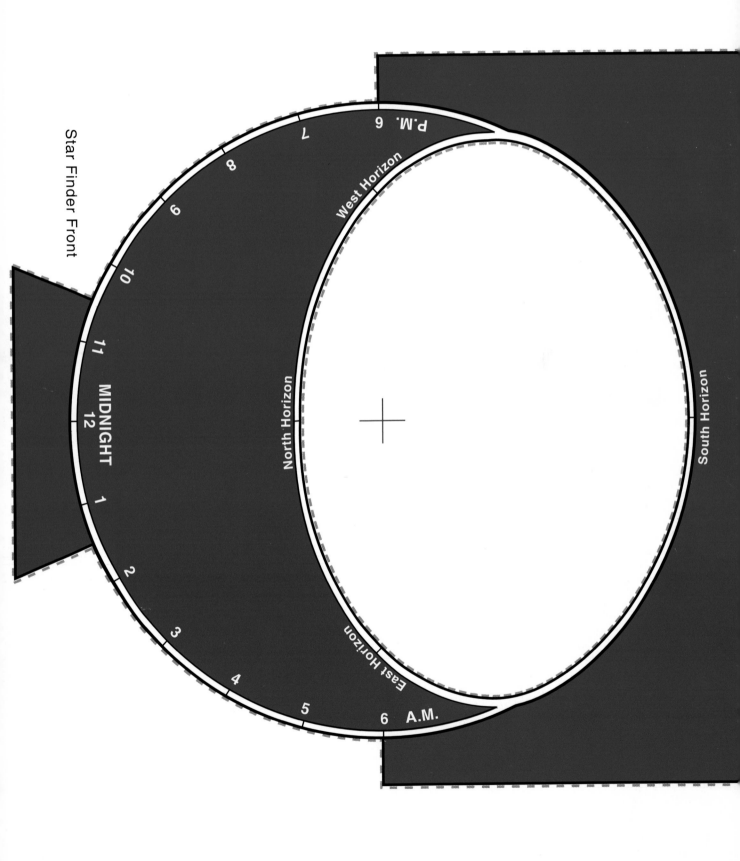

Star Finder Front

P.M.
6
7
8
9
10
11
12 MIDNIGHT
1
2
3
4
5
6 A.M.

West Horizon
North Horizon
East Horizon
South Horizon

The Rotating Star Finder

To make your Rotating Star Finder, you need a pair of scissors, clear tape, and a paper clip or a small piece of wire.

1. Cut out the round constellation disc and the long blue viewfinder along the blue dotted lines only, including the oval in the middle. This is the window in which you will find the constellations.

2. Lay the viewfinder on a flat surface with the blue color facedown. Fold the viewfinder along the thick black dotted line, so the halves match up exactly. Then slip the disc between the two pieces, with the constellations showing through the viewfinder window.

3. Align the bottom edges of the viewfinder and tape them together. In the center of the constellation disc, find the blue star in Ursa Minor. With an adult's help, poke a small hole in this star and through the back. Make sure that the rounded area of the days on the constellation disc aligns with the hour timeline on the front of the viewfinder.

4. Stick a paper clip or a small piece of wire through the hole so that no more than ½ inch shows through the front. Bend that piece over to keep the wire from slipping through the hole. Repeat on the other side, bending the wire to keep the star finder pieces together. Put a small piece of tape over the wire on the back side.

5. Look at pages 13 through 17 of *The Ultimate Guide to the Sky* for directions on how to use your Rotating Star Finder.

Tape here

Star Finder Back

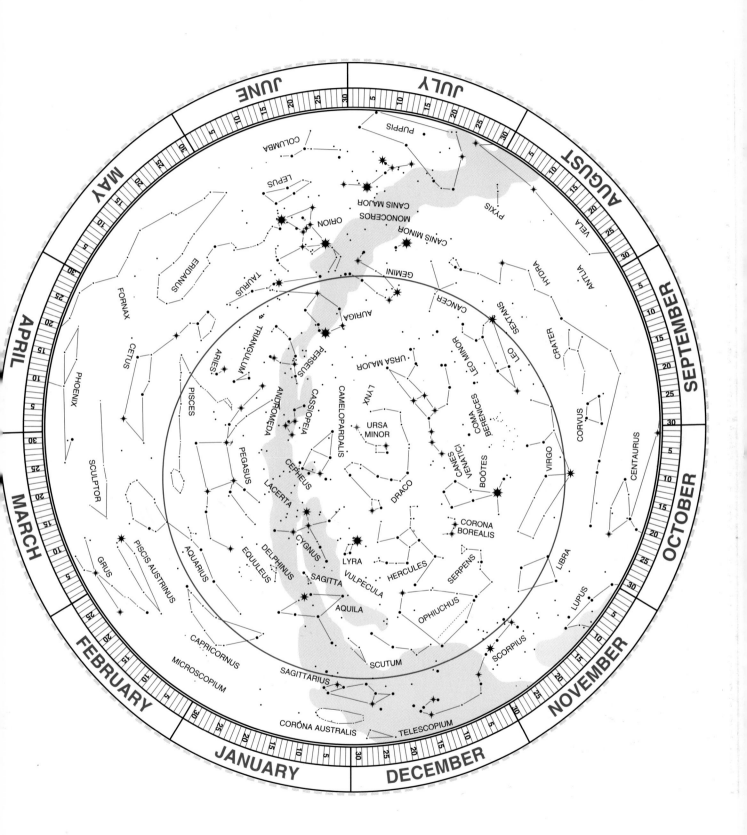